knock

AND TEACHING

A seven-year manual for

primary/elementary teaching

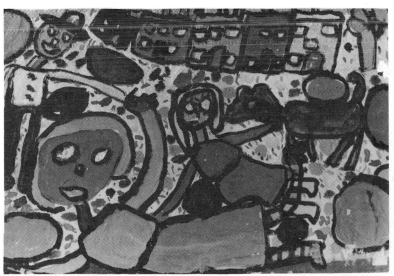

'Dog knocks down two girls.' Shape and line. Age: 8.

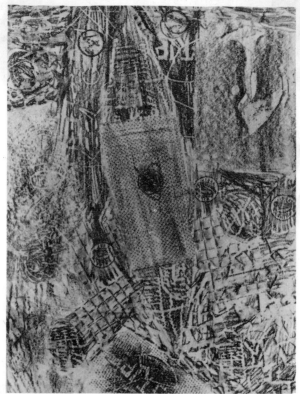

'The Rocket.' Expression through rubbings. Age: 9.

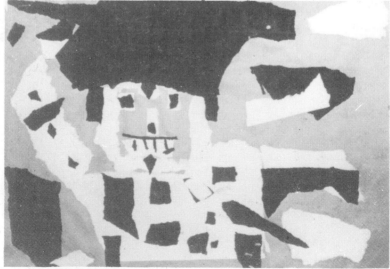

'The Pirate.' Torn paper picture. Age: 8.

Art Learning and Teaching

A seven-year manual for the
primary/elementary teacher

DIARMUID LARKIN

WOLFHOUND PRESS

Published with the generous support of
An Chomhairle Ealaíon (The Arts Council)

British Library Cataloguing in Publication Data

Larkin, Diarmuid
    Art learning and teaching.
      1. Art – Study and teaching (Elementary)
      I. Title
    372.5'044   N350

ISBN 0-9503454-5-8   1/12/84

Published by
Wolfhound Press
98 Ardilaun, Portmarnock,
County Dublin, Ireland.

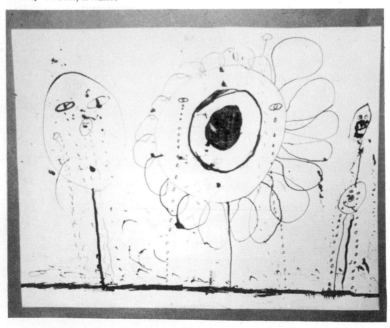

'Crying Flower.' Pen and ink drawing. Empathy. Age: 9.

CONTENTS

ACKNOWLEDGEMENTS

Photographs are supplied by the author unless otherwise credited in the text or here. The author and the publisher both acknowledge the unnamed creators of the examples of child art reproduced in this book, many of which have been collected by the author over several years. We are very grateful to the administrators of the Texaco Child Art Competition for permission to reproduce some award winning entries. Line illustrations are by **Jeanette Dunne** and, on pages 179, 192, 193, 202, 203, 204, 212, 243 and 244, by Redsetter Ltd. for the publisher. Illustrations on page 214 are by the author. Photographs are by the author or as credited except: those on pages 29, 32, 49, 78, 84, 115, 117, 134, 147, 160, 185, 199 and 239 and colour photographs pages 79 bottom; 98 top and left; 101 mid-right and bottom left are by **Eilish Ryan**; on page 157 by Michael Cashman; and on pages 83, 124 and 133 courtesy Source Archives, Dublin. We are grateful in addition to Redsetter Ltd. and Eilish Ryan for additional photographic processing. Design is by Seamus Cashman of Wolfhound Press, and layout by Redsetter Ltd. Cover design is by Jarlath Hayes.

PREFACE

It is hoped that these exemplary learning situations will be taken only as a guide when working out an art programme.

The learning experiences are developed in sequence advancing from simple to complex so that the art experiences will help the child to develop an understanding of the art elements and principles of design, thereby establishing habits of creativity as part of every day life.

I would like to express my appreciation to all those who have made this book possible. The bibliography acknowledges the main publications which I have used as points of reference. I owe much to the many children, student teachers, art teachers and colleagues who have worked with me down through the years. I am particularly indebted to those children whose work I have used as illustrations.

My acknowledgement is also due to Seamus Cashman of the Wolfhound Press for his encouragement and patience.

Diarmuid Larkin
Carysfort College of Education
Blackrock, County Dublin

Note: Numbers given in brackets in the text of a lesson relate to the numbered items in that lesson under the heading 'Learning'.

Average Class / Age / Grade

Junior Infants	Age	4/ 5	Kindergarten
Infants		5/ 6	Grade 1
First Class		6/ 7	Grade 2
Second Class		7/ 8	Grade 3
Third Class		8/ 9	Grade 4
Fourth Class		9/10	Grade 5
			Intermediate / Junior High
Fifth Class		10/11	Grade 6
Sixth Class		11/12	Grade 7
—		12/13	Grade 8

INTRODUCTION

In this book the teacher in the primary school classroom or indeed any parent of young children will find a series of involvement situations ranging from the simple to the complex which are designed to help them challenge the mental and personal development of the child. Areas for exploration are suggested — perceptual awareness, restricted response, evaluation and appreciation, manipulation and control. Learning situations which involve these areas follow a logical progression of discovery starting with the child's reaction to the world around him (child orientated rather than process orientated) and developing to a stage where the child is beginning to evaluate these reactions and is able to use them in a positive way, i.e. relating his learning in the classroom to the world outside.

In the last eighty years we have witnessed a continuum of change in the issues that shape and mould our understanding of what constitutes Art now. These issues, by and large, are reflected in the changes of emphasis which contribute and enlarge the nature of art education to-day.

In this country we are becoming aware of the change from the deterministic approach, i.e. development of skills without providing any opportunity for the child to use these skills in art experiences that involve creative thinking, to a more enlightened art education where the child's awareness of his own experiences are utilised for creative expression.

The common misunderstanding in art education is the misconception that isolated end-product or process-orientated activities with media constitute an effective art programme in relation to the child.

Media skills are of no great value until the child achieves a knowledge of and insight into the subject under consideration. The acquisition of skills should be related to the needs of the child. The misconception happens when skill in art (e.g. the ability to use tools and media to carry out certain processes — making rubbings, cutting and tearing tissue paper etc.) is treated in isolation from the equally important skills that relate to 'means' rather than 'ends'; knowing, seeing, feeling must be integrated within the doing.

The child evolves a product as one aspect in a range of experiences that reflect his total experience. The emphasis on this end product, rather than on the learning processes does not give the child the opportunity to enrich his individual awareness and understanding of the world of nature and man. An increased development of the sensory mechanism, e.g. learning to observe, listen, touch, smell, develops the child's powers of perceptual and critical observation thus helping him to explore, express and relate the different relationships in his world.

In his art expression the child tries to develop an ability to say and tell ideas which are inventive and personal. What are needed therefore are involvement situations which 'motivate' the child's emotional, intellectual and perceptual powers in a creative way. As Victor Lowenfeld aptly said in *The Creative and Mental Growth of the Child*: "Unless we penetrate into an experience whatever its nature may be, it will remain superficial and cannot serve as a basis for creativity."

Every teacher who teaches art in the classroom is responsible for the vitality of the art programme through his preparation, knowledge and methods of teaching and through his effective use of the time available for art within the curriculum. The teacher must motivate the child to establish the habit of creativity and to this end develop a framework, i.e. a sequential art programme within which learning in Art and Design is based. Motivation is, in effect, winding up the mainspring for awareness, creativity and individual potential. Educationally, we are slotting in on the natural behaviour of the child, and at the same time we are motivating him in a way that is parallel to this development. The child therefore is becoming aware through his own senses.

Children who are exposed to a wide range of sensory experience are more likely to be self-assured. Through regular repetition and reinforcement of the child's natural experiences, he builds concepts about himself and his environment, and the relationships between the concepts of art are realised.

In the art programme at the primary level the child naturally uses the conceptual content as outlined in the Structure of the Programme Model for Art Education (see below). This includes the art elements, the principles of design and the historical references. In working with these art elements the teacher helps the child to produce unity in his visual expressions. The child's art experiences therefore should cater for a more heightened sensitivity to a variety of textures, colours, shapes and forms. Many possibilities for experience-orientated art learning can be gained from sensory awareness when one considers all the smells, sounds, and body movements, and the many variations that are possible. This approach in education helps the child to become aware of his own instinctive behaviours as a 'source-bank' of stimuli.

If we are concerned with the growth and development of an individual human being, we are dealing with problems that are highly subjective and unquestionably unique. This personal growth or self-discovery of the individual could be opened up through his art learning. There has been a tendency to apply the more accepted methods that relate to academic subjects to art teaching, but it must be remembered that art deals with the daily behaviours of the child, and as such it is multi-sensory. This multi-sensory involvement expands perception, and as an approach to education it has implications which are as unlimited as man's own capacities for self-realisation. This capacity for multi-sensory perception is common to all children, but appears to be rare among adults. As adults the emphasis to our way of life conditions us to perceive through a linear, *particular*, approach rather than a multi-sensory, continuous, all-at-once, relationship with our environment.

A linear empirical approach influences our perceptions so strongly as to constrict our experience of our environment in a multi-sensory way. Those who retain this multi-sensory ability are usually found to be artists or others with exceptional aesthetic sensitivity. However as educationalists we are not catering solely for an artistic elite, but for all children. Helping them to make their experiences become relevant to themselves, and to a society such as ours, enables them to deal also with the growing use of visual art forms in the man media.

MOTIVATION

Motivation is a very important part of the learning situation. Children need help in their thinking. They need to be excited about their ideas in order to re-create them through an art medium. They need to recall experiences vividly. They must be sufficiently wound-up to give them a desire to communicate this in visual terms.

Motivation is also a way by which the child can be helped to think through an idea and re-live his experiences.

There are different approaches that could be used:

Verbal Discussion: This should take place before and after every experience.

Visual Experience: This occurs when the teacher presents slides, photographs, films.

Direct Experience: This means the child takes part in an actual event, e.g. walking through the yard, a building, a greenhouse, working in the garden, visiting the park, etc.

Material Experience: Paint is experimented with on a surface. The manipulation of the pigment could suggest possibilities for investigation. Working with clay could be a way of discovering possibilities before starting to make an object.

Sensory Experience: This is responding to 'outside' information through the senses. In this the child can increase his awareness of the world around him through his auditive, tactile, and olfactory senses.

Developing Perceptive Awareness: A good general approach is to direct attention to objects in the environment (e.g. a nature trip, or the teacher could ask the children to collect natural forms which they could then examine and see what can be discovered).

The following is a suggested structure model for a Sequential Programme to serve the teacher and through him the pupil.

```
                    ┌─────────────────────┐
                    │  THE ENVIRONMENT    │
                    └─────────────────────┘
                              ↕
                          NATURAL
                              ↕
                         MAN-MADE
                              ↓
                          OTHERS
                              ↑
                    ┌─────────────────────┐
                    │     THE CHILD       │
                    └─────────────────────┘
                              ↓
                 FUNCTIONS OF THE ORGANISM
```

INTELLECT EMOTIONS MOTOR INSTINCT

↓	↓	↓
PERCEPTUAL AWARENESS	SEEING	Develops Powers of Critical Observation
AESTHETIC RESPONSE	FEELING	Appreciates and Develops Sensitivity to Aesthetic Values
EVALUATION APPRECIATION	THINKING	Objective Evaluation and Personal Discrimination
MANIPULATION OF TOOLS AND MATERIAL	DOING	Gives Visual Form to Emotions, Ideas, and Feelings

↓

ART ELEMENTS	ART MEDIA	PRINCIPLES OF DESIGN	HISTORICAL ELEMENTS
Line	Drawings	Balance	Development
Shape	Painting	Movement	and styles
Form	Collage	Variety	
Colour	Graphics	Unity	
Texture	Ceramics		
Space	Crafts		

```
┌─────────────────────────────────────────────────────┐
│        ESTABLISHING INTER-RELATIONSHIPS             │
│  VISUAL ARTS    MUSIC    ARCHITECTURE    DRAMA      │
└─────────────────────────────────────────────────────┘
```

As the structure of the Programme Model suggests the Art Programme should bring about a change in the child's behaviour in the following areas:-

1. Perceptual Awareness
2. Aesthetic Response

3. Expression, Manipulation and Control
4. Evaluation and Appreciation

These headings need further amplification:

1. *What is Perceptual Awareness?*

It is developing in the child an ability to see and understand the *visual relationships* in and around his environment. This type of learning starts with the child's curiosity about the everyday things and events which affect him. It is important to lead the child into experiences, but also to let him discover things for himself. He must perceive his environment in his own way, e.g. in an experience in his everyday life; *awareness* is making that experience become conscious; the child observes, identifies, compares, contrasts, relates the visual relationships which form the total impression.

In summary, sensory perception is a way of perceiving through the senses. In this way we are developing within the child an ability to deal with his world as a series of multi-sensory events. The purpose of his art education at this level is to help him integrate those experiences and to relate them to himself in a way that is in keeping with his own natural growth and development as a person.

2. *Aesthetic Response*

While vision seems to be the most common method by which learning takes place, there are other areas of sensory learning which vision alone cannot capture. This area of learning develops in terms of his senses and capacity for empathy. The child is encouraged through his faculty for empathy to become aware of sensory qualities as things in themselves, e.g. sights, sounds, tastes, tactile surfaces, forms, colours, movement and space — each of which generates its own aesthetic response. The child develops a fuller understanding when he is receptive to his feelings and experiences and can take in new information and see things in new relationships. As he learns to respond to his environment through his art experiences, he learns to appreciate and enjoy the richness and diversity of nature.

3. *Expression-Manipulation and Control of Art Media and Processes*

Expression is a result of thoughts and feelings that are developed according to the child's reactions to his experiences. Experience includes his reactions to external environment, natural and man-made, as well as his internal reactions, emotions, dreams, fantasies, etc. The various media and processes function as the 'means' through which the child gives concrete form to these experiences, while the art elements are the means that help the child externalise them. Expression therefore, goes beyond the area of subject matter to the area of tools and materials used. The art programme should

12

equip the child with manipulative skills in saying things with art materials. Experience with materials can open up a range of expressive possibilities. The teacher must plan many art experiences so that the child develops a *fluency and flexibility with a few* of these tools and media as well as *a depth of experience in one*. The child also must be encouraged to select the tools and media most suitable to him to express his ideas and feelings.

4. *Evaluation and Appreciation*

Related to visual and sensory sensitivity, which are the factors which motivate expression, is the area of the child's ability to become aware of the consequences of his experiences in art, i.e. appreciation.

This area not only helps the child to develop a language for establishing values in his own art work and the art work of others (art criticism), but also includes collecting information about his cultural heritage (art history). Critical perception goes beyond simple perceptual training in that it deals with values. It helps the child develop a visual vocabulary for looking at qualities in his environment.

To develop awareness of his now found abilities, questions must be directed towards helping him relate his own art experiences to the art experiences of others, e.g. the art of his class group, of his environment, and of other cultures. This gives the child the opportunity to talk about his work, to verbalise his learning and thereby reinforce what learning has happened.

Information received from this discussion helps both the teacher and the child to set future situations that will expand and direct the learning further.

HELPING THE CHILD TO RELATE THROUGH HIS SENSE IMPRESSIONS

As far as creative development in the child is concerned the senses must be activated and to this end the child's experience plays a very important role. A greater understanding and depth of awareness can be brought about by helping the child to *recall* his experiences and by drawing his attention to what he already knows.

This can be done by asking questions that will help the child to recall in vivid detail thoughts, perceptions and feelings derived from his experiences, e.g. if the experience was an emotional experience he would be asked to recall how he 'felt' — how he felt when he was nearly knocked down by a car? How excited he was when he was going on holidays? How sad he felt when his dog was run over? How happy he was on his birthday? How angry he was when his bicycle was stolen?

Of course his experiences can be sometimes more physical in nature, and therefore common, such as a headache, a bad cut on his knee, twisting his ankle, falling from a tree. These are experiences that he has gone through and been part of, and because of this he is able to relate to these readily and can express his reactions to them in his art activities.

Another way of developing awareness is to get the child to relate to the object, that is to get him to identify with the object in the sense that he becomes the object — empathy. To gain an understanding of empathy and to increase the child's understanding of it, and also stretch his imagination, a situation must be devised where the child can relate to the object with which he is identifying.

An example of this would be imagining himself as a tree. The following points might be checked:

Feel the sun shining on you
Feel the snow on your head
Feel the rain beating on you
Are your feet stuck in one position or can you move around?
How do you move in a storm?
Have ivy choke you, and insects crawl over you.

In this type of experience the child uses many of his senses, i.e. he takes part in an integrated multi-sensory experience. As the child develops through these experiences he becomes more visually acute and he begins to seek experiences that channel his awareness in a way that goes from the general to the particular.

The child in other words should be encouraged to look at his environment, and 'see' it in terms of his senses; to select from what he sees by establishing relationships between what he 'sees' and 'feels' and what aspects make up his experience; and to 'express' or put down in a visible form what he *relates to* from his experience. For example, what is the line doing? What range of marks can be made with the pencil, crayon, brush etc.? How suitable is the mark made to the idea or feeling he wants to *express*? How and what meaning does he give to the marks that he has discovered initially from his environment?

AESTHETIC SENSITIVITY

Aesthetic sensitivity is essential to perceive and value the things we see, hear and touch within the natural and man-made environment. There is more to aesthetics than appreciating art works in galleries. There is the satisfaction derived from our perception of aesthetic qualities, such as form, colour, texture and their combinations disassociated from descriptive content in our common experiences with things and events. Unless we have a developed sensitivity to the aesthetic, we cannot fully appreciate man's perception, i.e. the influences that mould and shape his interpretation of his world.

14

Throughout man's creative endeavours we see reflected, emotions and ideas which are associated with the underlying social and cultural changes current to his time and place. These factors play an important part in shaping and influencing man's mode of feeling and thinking, since every era develops its own language symbols or visual metaphors for expressing its perception of change that is particular to its time.

Aesthetic Awareness and the Child

All children have a capacity for perceiving and this is evidenced in their art work. Also children have a capacity for reacting to art, but this must be developed. Provision must be made to allow the child to react to art in his art learning apart from his own personal involvement in making.

In helping the child become familiar with art works he can realise that the adult artist is expressing emotions, ideas, and experiences similar to his own, with the qualification that the level of understanding is different. Assisting the child to discuss the art forms of adult artists gives encouragement to his own creative efforts and develops his verbal skills in expressing opinions about his own art work and the art work of others in his class group.

ART APPRECIATION AND THE CHILD

An empathic approach to introduce the child to art forms could be used. This approach involves the child in identifying himself with the particular art form under review, by putting himself in the place and time of the artist in order to recognise and to understand something about how it was made (i.e. materials and processes used) and its function (i.e. accessories to dance, drama, religious ceremonies, adornment, decoration, design or communication projects).

The child projects his reactions or feelings into the art form, and interprets it (expressive content) in his own way. While the child is projecting his own emotions and feelings into the art work he is at the same time deriving meaning from it by comparing, recognising and forming opinions about what the artist does, how he does it, and why.

The provision of art appreciation in the programme need not be a difficult task. It could be planned in the following manner. Emphasis could be based for the first, second and third classes on how man has made use of the art elements. Emphasis could be based for the fourth and fifth classes on developing empathic situations where the child imagines himself in the place and time of the artist, and learns about different styles in art brought about by the different cultures. Emphasis could be based for the sixth class on learning more about individual artists, what they expressed, and how they expressed it.

AESTHETICS AND THE ENVIRONMENT

To-day there is a growing awareness of the lack of distinctness and clarity existing in our environment. There are of course many types of environments apart from the urban and natural landscape, which 'work on' us both internally (our personal experience of 'things' in the context of time and space) and externally (our reference to the physical world of objects). These influences man tries to assimilate and extracts qualities which we call aesthetic.

Aesthetics require certain consciousness which has to be developed. We all possess the ability to conceptualise about our environment. It is this ability that enables man to exist despite the apparent complexity and fragmented events of man and nature. In order to control his environment, man has to think logically, to categorise, to look for a rationality and order, to manipulate his environment in an efficient and deliberate way.

Because we are the victims of our own compartmentalisation, we cannot easily integrate or make the connections between the segmented parts of our lives and our relationship to our world. Now more than ever, we need to know who we are, where we are, and where we want to go. With the power of connection we cut ourselves off from our direct experience, and live in a world of abstractions. It is clear that man's ability to conceptualise cannot answer all his needs; for instance, when confronted with a chair, if we see it in terms of ideas, rather than a direct experience of it, our consciousness of it remains in a conceptual realm. We find that we already know a lot about it because we put it in the category 'chair' — we know its function — the size relationships of its parts, its colour etc. But there is something more about the chair, however slight, that is unique; maybe it is its texture, or the grain in the timber, something that never existed before and never will exist again. The type of consciousness that we use conceptually is not the same as the type of consciousness we develop when appreciating something in an aesthetic way. If one confines one's observation to a conceptual level, one only notices the qualities of the chair that make it resemble all other chairs. But when one begins to notice these qualities that make the chair itself, then one is seeing the chair through an aesthetic consciousness.

Many children will not be art producers, but they will be consumers. As consumers they will affect their environment and will be affected by it. It is hoped that an understanding of the function of art will enable them to affect their environment with discernment. The child's art learning, if it is to be relevant, must help him to develop a critical attitude to his surroundings. To this end, opportunities should be provided for children to explore ideas and discover our natural and man-made environment.

Environmental and aesthetic education can be started at a very early age in the child's life. The most important environment for him is his home and his neighbourhood, his journey to and from school. These situations provide many starting points for motivating the child to develop a greater perception of the natural and man-made things in his surroundings. A closer look at his world can help develop a greater awareness which at the same time helps him to be more discriminating about the objects that make up his environment.

Children in the first and second class could be taken on a scenic walk. Focus could be made on the natural elements of the school and home such as trees, bushes, rock, and sky. Children could be asked to perceive and identify these things which surround them and are too often missed.

A discussion of colours, shapes and textures they have seen can be followed up by drawing and painting experiences. Each child can express his own personal ideas and experiences. Group projects such as a collective painting could help them to share ideas and work with one another.

In the third and fourth classes, art activities could be expanded to provide a better understanding of concepts and skills involved; as the boundaries of his experiences expand a closer look could be taken of the local community. The objects in his surroundings, i.e. buildings, streets, doorways, chimneys, street furniture, parks, playgrounds, recreation areas, could help him to develop a concern about the conditions and to learn what he can contribute to improve its aesthetic quality.

In the fifth and sixth classes, children must be asked many questions which provoke discussion; what makes the place interesting, what is it that is appealing about the landscape, what has man contributed to its aesthetic appearance (e.g. which buildings should be preserved and which buildings should be torn down and why).

Such discussions can provide a basis for many meaningful art activities. Environmental education is of a great concern to us all today. Since the quality of the environment could deteriorate at a rapid pace, we must assume some responsibility for educating children in the primary schools to take an active critical role in their environment. Children must be taught to see the aesthetic relationships in art forms that man has created as well as in natural forms. Ecology and art are partners. Children can become aware of the many dimensions of ecology through creative art teaching, and, through this, they can be made more aware of their role in our ever changing society.

SPACE, PERCEPTION AND EXPRESSION

Space is a natural human experience. It is not merely something out there, outside ourselves, from which we are isolated. When we experience space, we position ourselves in that space, and from our position we can move up – down – right – left, forwards and backwards. This space is three-dimensional in that it exists all around us.

17

Artists, in trying to describe the sense of space, have come up with many different solutions. In the European Renaissance, artists developed perspective, which was a geometric system of vanishing points, in which parallel lines meet in the distance. We have seen this happen with railway tracks. This became a framework for representing semi-realism as an ultimate in visual reality. This particular space concept was frozen as it was based upon a fixed viewpoint, eliminating the element of time and change and meant that the spectator was on the outside 'looking in'. In direct opposition to this the Eastern artist expressed space with an inverse perspective, where lines expanded from the spectators' point of view to an almost infinite distance, i.e. the spectator identified himself as being in the space as opposed to looking through a window.

The Byzantines and the Persians represented spatial depth in a different way by using the device of overlapping images. In Western art during the seventeenth and eighteenth centuries space was represented by amplifying forms and creating distortions, introducing dramatic gestures, and focusing on single elements within the composition. Here light became the determining factor in moulding and shaping the space within the picture surface.

Today the artist is freed from the imitative representation of space by mechanical inventions such as the camera, film, and television. He is free to express himself in terms of his own time and place. The image becomes a dynamic experience, instead of a dead inventory of optical facts, where he expresses the spatial experience of his own generation.

When we perceive space, we relate to it through our own body existence, i.e. we are taking part in a person-thing relationship which we order, to make sense out of, and we express or communicate this spatial orientation. In a sense we interrelate with space, and this space affects us as much as we affect it. An example is the use we make of the space within a room; we can expand or contract it by altering the sizes, positions, directions of the furniture we place within it. Many of us would be surprised, however, if someone told us that we had just taken part in a spatial configuration!

Most people are familiar with actual space and with the visual cues we use either consciously or intuitively to control and adjust our orientation to space. When representing or expressing space-tension on a two dimensional surface or in three dimensions certain perceptual factors influence the way we articulate the space. These are the factors of proximity and distance, convergence, progression and regression which are influenced by size, colour, position, direction, overlapping. These factors act as the means for adjusting our spatial framework and are common to both two-dimensional and three-dimensional space expression.

The extent of our receptivity to these factors enables us to express spatial depth in the plastic arts, painting, sculpture, music, drama, movement, architecture, etc. In creating spatial depth within a two-dimensional surface, we are not reproducing actual space, but making use of *spatial cues* that are common to our experience of actual space. By adjusting these cues to the requirements of a flat surface, further spatial tensions develop as soon as a mark is placed within that surface. All elements of composition — lines, spaces, colours, volumes — interact to set up space tensions (e.g. the relationship of hues, the distribution of accents, and the direction of lines). The quality of depth desired and achieved happens as a result of the artist's choice of elements and technique used. The contrast of elements affords space tensions, but what unites them is space resolution.

As already mentioned, in the work of both past and contemporary artists many devices both traditional and innovatory have been used for representing space and forms. The key question is: are these visual cues operative in terms of the child's learning? If the teacher is looking at the work of children with the perceptual assumptions of space which he has developed as an adult, he may erroneously judge the work in an unfair way, and miss out on the inventiveness of the child's solutions for representing space. To the child it is natural to fold up the space by combining plan view and elevations as in Egyptian art, or to combine many different eye levels within the one piece of work as in the use of one or more base lines, which may or may not be combined with cut-away or X-ray representation which conveys the idea of inside and outside.

COLOUR

Colour is a vital force in our lives, and can be used to bring out creative expression in children. Colour is also a hidden power that can sway our emotions and actions. For our knowledge of colour we are indebted to the research carried out by the chemist, physicist, psychologist and the artist. From their findings we know more about the power of colour and how it works, and the impact it has on people. We are beginning to make use of this knowledge in our surroundings by making a more enlightened use of colour. A creative use of colour can effectively bring about an environment which is more favourable to man's emotional, mental and spiritual activity.

Colour, like the air we breathe, surrounds us and is continually changing. Change is brought about by the reactions of colour to light, by the action of colours on nearby colours. Colours in our environment may have different surfaces and textures and are affected by distance and atmosphere. Identical colours applied to a glossy surface or to rough textile surface are quite different in appearance because they absorb and reflect light in a different way. Colour is affected by light conditions and under certain circumstances may tend to merge, e.g. at twilight all colours tend to become greyish.

Colours can create strong impressions on us, because our reactions can sometimes be influenced by our previous experience and memory of those colours. We experience colour with regard to the object world, and despite changes of illumination, colours can signify the colour of the object, e.g. coal is black, snow is white, the sky is blue, and an orange is orange. This type of vision is brought about by our sense of constancy and our related perception to colour is brought about not by our direct experience and receptiveness to actual colours, but by our generalisation of colour as a means of identifying forms in the environment.

Experiencing a colour in terms of its hue, value, intensity, becomes more than a means of 'labelling' in that it has an apparent size and weight. Yellow is seen as the largest of all hues, followed by white, orange, red, green, blue, black. The weight and size of a colour is useful in that applied to a room it can make it look bigger or smaller; in terms of weight, pale or light colours will appear less heavy than deep ones.

Colour has a definite effect on our emotions, in that it can activate our senses, it can be soothing or irritating, exciting or depressing. We often describe feelings in terms of colour, e.g. 'seeing red', 'feeling blue'. Colours can create a mood or feeling of sadness or happiness. Also some colours can 'explode' or 'vibrate', 'expand' and 'contract', 'advance' or 'recede'. This means that they project impulses which set up corresponding responses in the viewer which activate his senses.

There are many motivational factors that can be used to help children express themselves with colour. The following suggested experiences may stimulate new and further awareness, using paint as a material.

Dropping colours onto a wet surface and allowing them to run

Dripping melted crayons

Looking through a prism

Looking at a colour against a white background, and removing it to see the after-image

Placing tissues or cellophane over each other to mix colours.

There are many materials that could be used to introduce colour besides the more conventional art materials. The following could be experimented with: food dyes dropped into water mixed with paste, liquid shoe polish, coloured inks, tea, coffee, dyes made from fruit juices, fabric coldwater dyes, coloured pages from magazines, coloured poster paper, coloured tissue paper. Experiments with unusual materials should re-open the senses to conventional materials.

Questions which would help children identify colour and to see a wide range and contrast could be on the following lines:

Do you see colour when you close your eyes?

How many different greens do you see from where you are sitting?

Both of these objects are red, but they are different reds, do you know why?

Is the sky always blue?

How many different whites do you see in the paper?

Is there any difference in colour between the object near you and the one far away?

Do we wear dull clothes or bright clothes?

At an early stage the child's use of colour is spontaneous, and therefore only a few colours are needed, say three or four. The colours can be prepared separately in jars with appropriate brushes for each colour. This eliminates to a great extent the possibility of spilling the water.

The Colour Wheel.

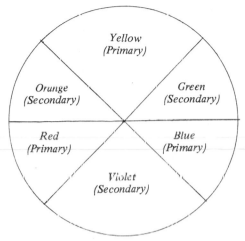

THE GRAMMAR OF ART

To bring about change in the pupils' behaviour in art they must have an understanding of the grammar of art.

Art Elements and *Principles of Design* are made use of to convert ideas into pictorial form, to create design, pattern, space and depth.

Understanding line as an ART ELEMENT

Line is shape producing
Line can create the illusion of going into and coming out of an area
Line can portray rhythm
Line can be expressive
Line can be used to divide area, separate spaces
Surface lines can indicate form without shading
Multiple similar lines become texture.

Understanding shape as an ART ELEMENT

Shape is two-dimensional
Shape can identify a familiar object
Shape can denote importance through contrast of large and small
Shape can indicate movement
Shape can create pattern
Shape can be negative or positive
Shape can be regular or free form

21

Understanding form as an ART ELEMENT
Form is a three-dimensional
Form is seen as mass or volume
Form occupies space
Form casts a shadow when light is played on it
Form can be a cup, a boat, a house or a tree

Understanding colour as an ART ELEMENT
Colour seen in art materials is called pigment
Colour is observed when light is refracted by a prism or absorbed and reflected by pigment
Colour can be mixed for effect
Colour can give a feeling of warm and cold
Colour gives the illusion of advancing and receding – warm colours advance; cold colours recede
Colour can be used to express emotion
Colour can have a symbolic meaning

COLOUR DIMENSION
1. HUE   The classification or name of a colour.
2. TONE   The lightness or darkness of a colour.
3. INTENSITY   The brightness or dullness of a colour.

PRIMARY COLOURS
Yellow, Red, Blue These can not be made by mixing.
SECONDARY COLOURS
Orange, Green, Violet are the mixture of two primary colours.
TERTIARY COLOURS
Olive, Russet, Citron are the mixture of two secondary colours.
NEUTRAL COLOURS
Black, Grey, White
COMPLEMENTARY COLOURS
Opposites on the colour wheel which create a maximum contrast Red-Green, Orange-Blue, Yellow-Violet
ANALOGOUS
Colours side by side on the colour wheel.
CHROMA
Refers to the saturation of the hue. E.g. Yellow may have an orange or green tint.
TEXTURE
Texture is the tactile surface quality of matter.
Texture can be two or three dimensional.
Texture can add variety and interest.
Texture is the application of the media in such a way as to depict a rough, smooth or broken surface.
Texture may be natural – such as tree bark.

Texture may be man made — glass, cloth.
Texture may be simulated — photographic illusion.
Texture in drawing — the way the pupil manipulates the tool affects the texture represented.

PRINCIPLES OF DESIGN

BALANCE refers to the visual or implied equality of like or unlike elements or forces.

SYMMETRY is formal balance.
ASYMMETRY is informal balance.

MOVEMENT refers to a means of leading the eye from one area to another in a work of art. A curved line gives different movement from a straight line.
RHYTHM refers to a regulated flow of art elements — they may be continuous, periodic, or alternating repetition.
VARIETY refers to elements and forces of different characteristics and qualities.

LINE AS AN ART ELEMENT

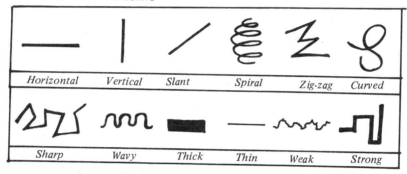

| Horizontal | Vertical | Slant | Spiral | Zig-zag | Curved |

| Sharp | Wavy | Thick | Thin | Weak | Strong |

SHAPE AS AN ART ELEMENT
Top: geometric.   Bottom: free form.

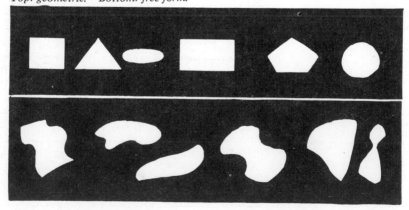

OPERATIONAL DESIGN

In the operational design the individual lesson is the learning situation in which the expected outcomes for the pupil are stated. It is also part of the major objectives of the overall art programme.

Stimulus No. 1

This is the source for the pupils' motivation i.e. what activates the learning are communicative transactions which may be primary, sensory, verbal and intellectual information.

Response/Stimulus 2

This consists of expressing through media, manipulating tools and making use of art elements and principles of design.

Response/Stimulus 3

The pupil is shaping personal standards, establishing the valuing processes, developing concepts about art and non art objects and events.

Expanding Opportunities

This simply is intended to provide a development and enrichment of the concepts in the learning situation.

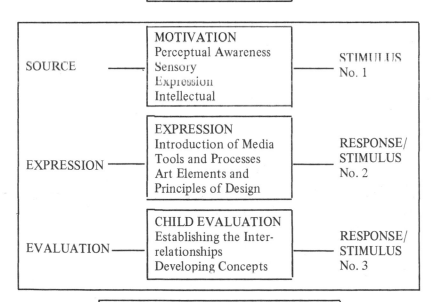

| INDIVIDUAL LESSON |
| (The Learning Situation) |

	MOTIVATION	
SOURCE ———	Perceptual Awareness Sensory Expression Intellectual	STIMULUS No. 1
EXPRESSION ———	EXPRESSION Introduction of Media Tools and Processes Art Elements and Principles of Design	RESPONSE/ STIMULUS No. 2
EVALUATION———	CHILD EVALUATION Establishing the Inter- relationships Developing Concepts	RESPONSE/ STIMULUS No. 3

| EXPANDING OPPORTUNITIES |
| ESTABLISHING FURTHER LEARNING |

INFANTS

Art Growth Characteristics

1. Ego-centred; thinks of himself as the centre of his world.
2. Control of scribbling; naming his scribblings.
3. Naming occurs when image has taken shape.
4. No understanding of object-space relation.
5. Includes only the parts that are meaningful to him.
6. Colour has an emotional appeal.
7. No understanding of relationship between colour and object.
8. Expresses mainly the movement (kinesthetic or muscular association).
9. Drawings do not depend on what is seen.
10. Objects and people do not appear realistically.
11. Control over line direction is developing.
12. Knows when the drawing is finished.
13. Attention span is short.
14. Time concept is now.

Behavioural Objectives (intended outcomes for the pupil)

The pupil will be able to:
Identify colours
Understand and identify textures
Identify repetition and rhythm
Understand similarities and differences in shape
Organise and arrange shapes
Understand dark and light
Identify the part of the whole
Understand pattern
Understand balance
Understand the difference between regular and irregular shapes
Understand dominant and subordinate shapes
Express movement and feeling

The pupil will gain control of and manipulate the following media and tools:
Paint with crayons
Cut, arrange and paste paper shapes
Develop a colour mosaic
Create three-dimensional forms
Construct with three-dimentional forms
Take impressions by rubbing
Simple printing by stamping
Manipulate plasticine or clay

INFANTS

Learning Situations
1. Expressing different movements through line.
2. Sorting and understanding hard and soft surfaces.
3. Feeling objects without seeing them and expressing them in line.
4. Recalling a textural quality and expressing it in line.
5. Organising line and colour in space.
6. Discovering that boxes have different faces and alike faces, big and small.
7. Discovering repetition and expressing it in line.
8. Finding new colours by mixing two or more colours.
9. Creating individual units of an idea and organising these shapes in an area.
10. Discovering colours can be dark and light.
11. Discovering balance with three dimensional forms.
12. Discovering the relationship of the parts to the whole in a three-dimensional construction.
13. Developing an understanding of tools and media.
14. Expressing an idea in colour.
15. Creating patterns with repetitive shapes.
16. Discovering variation in surface quality.
17. Using flat shapes to express an object.
18. Discovering the difference between regular and irregular shapes.
19. Creating lines which express movement.
20. Discovering that hands can smooth clay and make impressions in it.
21. Developing the ability to reorganise ideas using dominant and subordinate coloured shapes.
22. Experimenting with finger painting.
23. Developing an understanding of space organisation.
24. Forming with clay to establish an understanding of volume.

LEARNING SITUATION: Expressing different movements through line

PROCESS: Drawing with crayon

MATERIALS: Rubber ball, crayons or felt markers, newsprint

LEARNING: Perceiving Movement:

1. Vertical Lines
2. Horizontal Lines
3. Oblique Lines
4. Rolling in continuous and circular movements
5. Relating

MOTIVATION: A rubber ball is bounced on the floor. Question individual pupils: What way is the ball moving? Can you show me with your finger?

Newsprint and crayon are distributed to each pupil. They are now asked to show the movement on the paper with crayon (1). Question: Can the ball move any other way? The ball may be thrown from side to side or rolled (2). Again show the movement with the finger and crayon on the paper. Question: Are there any other ways to move the ball? The ball may be bounced against the wall. Show the finger and show on the paper (3).

A new sheet of paper is now distributed and pupils are asked to put the lines discovered together so that they will tell a story.

EVALUATION: Individual pupils are asked to tell the story of their pictures to the class. Question: Can we find the lines that go up and down in the class room (5)? What other types of lines can we find in the class room (5)?

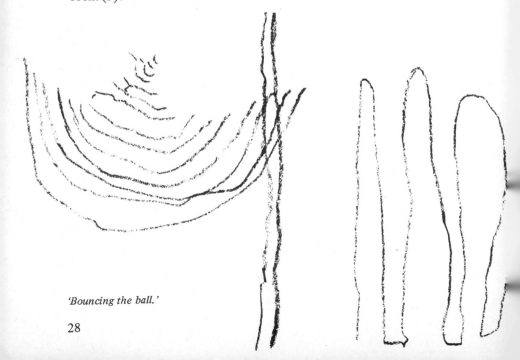

'Bouncing the ball.'

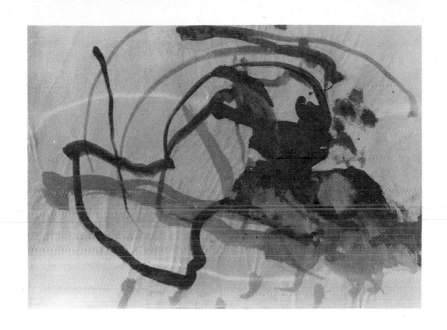

The Motor Act. Age: 4.

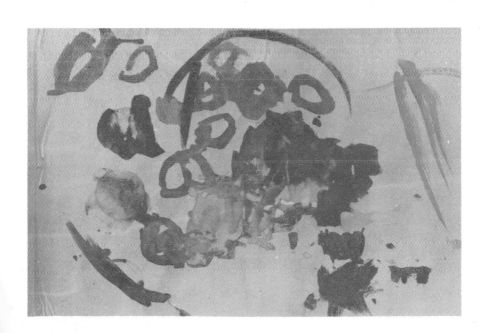

LEARNING SITUATION: Sorting and understanding hard and soft surfaces

PROCESS: Touching and selecting

MATERIALS: A wide range of objects with textures varying from hard to soft, e.g. sponges, cotton wool, feathers, knitting wool, fur, etc. contrasted with wood, metal, plastic, stones, cork, etc. A sheet of paper for support (format)

LEARNING: Sensory awareness/Textural qualities.

1. Arrangement and organisation
2. Contrasting textures
3. Relating different touch sensations to one another.

MOTIVATION: Distribute to each child two objects with soft and hard textural qualities. Question individual children: Do they both feel the same? What is the difference? Once the children are familiar with the words that describe the different textural sensations of the objects, they may be then asked to collect other contrasting hard and soft objects from a collection box and arrange (1) them on the format provided, making sure to place soft beside hard (2).

EVALUATION: Questions: How do all these objects feel when they are put together? Does the feel remind you of anything you have walked on? Can you show me anything else in the room that is hard, soft, etc? (This could be used to extend their vocabulary.) Do your hands tell you what the objects look like?

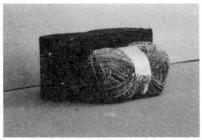

Texture: hard and soft.

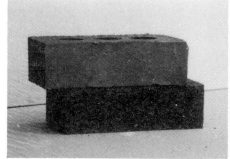

Texture: rough and smooth.

LEARNING SITUATION: Feeling objects without seeing them and expressing them in line

PROCESS: Drawing with crayons

MATERIALS: Paper bags containing rough and smooth objects to be distributed to each child. Newsprint 25 x 38cm approx. Assortment of coloured crayons

LEARNING: Sensory awareness/Textural qualities

1. Relating and recalling textural qualities
2. Vocabulary extension and extension of manipulative ability

MOTIVATION: After distributing to each child a bag containing contrasting textures, ask them to feel the objects in the bags without looking at them. Now can you tell about the differences that you found with your crayons instead of in words?

EVALUATION: Arrange a display of the children's drawings. Questions could be asked about the tactile qualities of the objects: What did the objects feel like? How rough? How smooth? Were there some that were neither rough nor smooth? Can you remember feeling anything else that felt like that (1)?

Refer to the drawings made: Can you find the rough and the smooth in the drawings? Ask individual children to identify the rough and smooth objects in their own drawings. How would you make the drawing rougher or smoother with your crayons (2)?

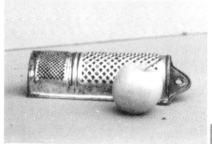

Texture: rough and smooth.

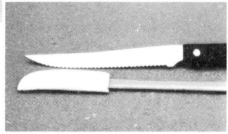

Texture: sharp and blunt.

LEARNING SITUATION: Recalling a textural quality and expressing it in line

PROCESS: Drawing

MATERIALS: Assorted coloured crayons. Newsprint support 38 x 25cm approx.

LEARNING: Recalling and expressing an experience

1. Relating the size of the shapes
   to the sheet of paper (format)

MOTIVATION: Let us make a picture of ourselves, but to make this picture we will have to remember how we felt when we walked on our bare feet.

Questions: Did you ever walk on your bare feet? What surface did you walk on? How did it feel? Was it rough, cold, sharp, hot, smooth? Did anybody ever walk on cold wet grass or on a hot footpath?

Tell me about yourself and how you felt with crayons on your sheet of paper. Don't forget to make yourself big on the paper (1).

EVALUATION: Arrange a display of the drawings. Questions could be asked about the drawings: Tell me how it felt? Is there any difference in how we feel when we walk on something rough and when we walk on something smooth? Are there other things that we could walk on that would make us feel different? Tell me about them?

Texture in the environment.

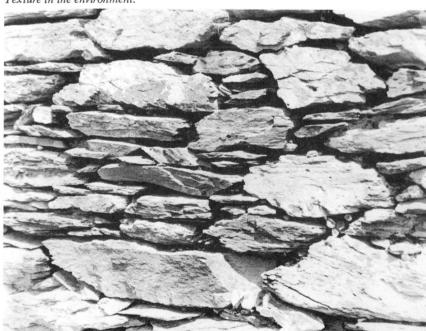

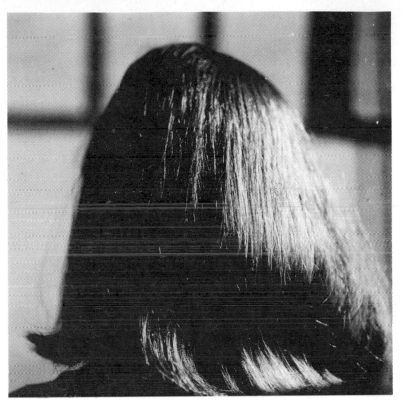

Texture and line.

Pattern — repetition in the environment.

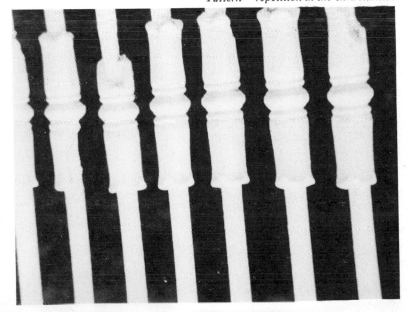

LEARNING SITUATION: To organise line and colour in space

PROCESS: Finger painting

MATERIALS: Tempera colour thickened with paste, cartridge paper for painting on, containers for the colour, papers for covering desks

LEARNING: Recalling a kinesthetic experience

1. Stating the problem
2. Organisation

3. Expressing a recalled experi- ence
4. Discovering a new colour by the mixing of two colours

MOTIVATION: How would you like to tell me about some movement you can remember?

Question: Did you ever watch birds flying? Tell how the birds moved. Does anybody know how a butterfly moves? How does a car move? Who can show me? What way does the rabbit move?

We will all show two movements on the paper with paints and your fingers (1).

Desks are covered with old newspapers (2). Cartridge paper is distributed. A spoonful of two contrasting colours are placed on each sheet of paper. Dip your finger in one colour first and make a picture of the movement you like best (3). When first movement is completed the pupils are asked to show another movement using the second colour.

When they have movements completed they may move one colour into the other to see what happens (4).

EVALUATION: Individual pupils are asked to hold up their paintings and are questioned: How did you feel when you were making the movement shown in the painting? Was it like anything else that happened to you? Show me in your painting where this is. What happened when the two colours moved together? (They changed.) When do you change move- ment? Are all movements the same? Does a baby move the same as a man?

EXPANDING OPPORTUNITIES: Painting the clown moving.

No.1 Finger Painting Base: Recipe	No. 2 Finger Painting Base: Recipe

1½ cups laundry starch
1 cup soap flakes (Lux)
1 quart of boiling water
	1 Package of cellulose wall-
	   paper paste
	1 Cup of soap flakes.
	   Boiling Water.

Make starch with a small amount of the boiling water. Add remaining boiling water and stir in soap flakes.	Add paste and boiling water to make a thick cream mixture.
Colour this base with food dyes.	This base may be added to liquid or powder tempera colour.

LEARNING SITUATION: Discovering that boxes have different faces and alike faces, big and small

PROCESS: Drawing and arranging shapes

MATERIALS: Crayons, newsprint, assortment of small boxes, e.g. match boxes, cigarette boxes, etc.

LEARNING:

1. Comparing relationships in shape
2. Stating the problem
3. Visual Vocabulary — Have we another name for the face?
4. Size relationships of shapes — large rectangular wall, small rectangular door, small rectangular book, small rectangular box beside the door. When the box is placed on the paper what happens?

MOTIVATION: Distribute the boxes amongst the children.

Question: Who can tell me how many faces are on the box? Are they all the same size (1)?

Let us find out what the big shape is like. (Demonstrate by placing the box on a sheet of paper and drawing a line around the contour with a crayon) (2). Draw all the faces on your box. Don't forget to place the big faces beside the small ones. What have we got? Can we name them? (Rectangles) (3). Draw some more rectangles now. Could you add more lines to them and make things out of them? If you like you may fill them in with different colours.

EVALUATION: Who would like to tell about what they made? Look and see what the big rectangle changed into. What about the small one? Are they lost in the big ones? How many were able to fill up the sheet of paper? What do we call the shape of the paper? Can we find more rectangles in the room (4)?

EXPANDING OPPORTUNITIES: A variety of shapes such as squares, rectangles and circles could be combined to create new shapes.

LEARNING SITUATION: Discovering repetition and expressing it in line

PROCESS: Drawing

MATERIALS: Newsprint, crayon or felt markers

LEARNING:

1. Direct experience
2. Vocabulary:
   (a) The word repetition is introduced
   (b) Stating the problem
3. This could be a starting point for developing simple patterns which could lead up to more complex patterns, e.g. border patterns
4. Verbalising
5. Relating

MOTIVATION: An individual pupil is asked to clap his hands, another is asked to walk and another is asked to swing his arms in and out (1).

Question: When you clap your hands do they move the same way all the time? When you swing your arms do they move the same way all the time? What do you call this (1)?

Sheets of newsprint and crayons are distributed. Pupils are asked to think of a movement (2). When they have thought of a movement they are asked to repeat it across the page in line from left to right. They are asked not to fill the page but to leave room for other movements. When the first movement is completed they are asked to try another one (3). Finally, they are asked to join two movements together.

EVALUATION: Individuals are asked to hold up their drawings (line patterns) and to talk about them (4).

Question: Can we find lines in the room that repeat themselves (5)? Where else would you find lines that repeat? – the railing, the windows, the desks, the grass etc.

EXPANDING OPPORTUNITIES: Expressing through swings, seesaws and running.

LEARNING SITUATION: Finding new colours by mixing two or more colours

PROCESS: Painting

MATERIALS: Tempera colours, brushes, sponges or fingers, large sheets of newsprint, jar of water and cleaning-up clothes

LEARNING: The behaviour of colour and their effects on each other

1. Stating the problem   2. Relating

MOTIVATION: Who would like to tell me the names of the colours? Who can find a red colour in the room? Are there any blue colours? What about yellow? How would you like to make colours? Does anybody know how they would do it?

Place three big blobs of yellow, red and blue on the paper, two near one another and one further away (1). (Demonstrate.) Let us see what happens when we move the blue into the yellow, the red into the yellow, the blue into the red. Now try putting them all together. Try making shapes with your new colours. Think what your picture is about.

EVALUATION: Who can name the new colours? Can we find the same colours in the room (2)? Maybe if we look out of the window we might find them also.

How many new colours did we find? How many do we know? Name them.

EXPANDING OPPORTUNITIES: Express taste through colour.

LEARNING SITUATION: Creating individual units of an idea and organising these shapes in an area

PROCESS: Arranging cut shapes

MATERIALS: Coloured paper (may be got from magazines), paper for support, scissors, paste, brushes and jars

LEARNING:

1. Recalling shapes
2. Arranging shapes
3. Number
4. Size relationships
5. Arrangement

MOTIVATION: How would you like to make a picture using different coloured shapes? Let us pretend it is a flower garden, and we are planting different flowers. We never saw these flowers before, they are imaginary flowers. We can make them with any shapes we like, think of the shapes we know. What are they (1)? Think of one shape. We will cut this out in the colour you like best. We will have to repeat this shape. How many will you make of it? Now put some paste on the back of them and stick them on the big sheet of paper. We will put them close together to make one big shape (2). Is this the flower? Why? What else have we to put in? (The stem — a straight line.) What else? (The leaves.) When we put them all together we have the flower. Now make some more flowers. Don't forget — the leaves, the stem, the petals.

EVALUATION: Did anybody put the same coloured flowers together? Count the number of flowers in your picture? How many leaves have you got (3)? Are some big and some small (4)? Did anybody put some near and some far away (5)?

EXPANDING OPPORTUNITIES: Drawing and arranging shapes found in the classroom and filling them in with various marks, dots and lines.

LEARNING SITUATION: Discovering colours can be dark and light

PROCESS: Mosaic, tearing and pasting

MATERIALS: Old magazines, cold water paste, a sheet of cartridge paper for support or heavy card

LEARNING:

1. Recognition of dark
2. Recognition of light
3. Relating
4. Discriminating in-between contrasts
5. Statement of the problem
6. Process demonstration
7. Procedure
8. Imagination

MOTIVATION: Who would like to tell me what dark is? Can a colour be dark? What is the opposite to dark (1)? Can we find light colours? Show me some in the room (2). When we place a light colour beside a dark colour, does the light colour change (3)? When we place a light colour on a light colour what happens (4)? (Demonstrate by placing a small light-coloured shape on a large coloured shape.) The small shape is lost. What did we find from this? If we place light on light, we cannot see the shape. What must we do? We can place light on dark or dark on light.

Old magazines are distributed, pupils are asked to find light and dark colours, tear out the colours and place all the dark together and all the light together (5). Put away the magazines. Now tear the colour pages into small shapes. Make neat heaps of each colour. Teacher demonstrates how to paste pieces on to the support (6). Each pupil is given a spoon of paste placed on a sheet of stiff card. The small coloured shapes are pressed on the paste and then pressed onto the support (7). How would you like to make a fierce animal with a lot of legs (8)? (Mosaic)

EVALUATION: How many made a picture with dark and light of one colour? Why did you use blue? Why red? Tell me about your animal. What makes him look fierce? How could we make him look kind? Is there any other way we could make him look?

LEARNING SITUATION: Discovering Balance with three-dimensional forms

PROCESS: Construction

MATERIALS: An assortment of boxes large and small, e.g. match boxes, cigarette boxes, etc., adhesive, cardboard for support

LEARNING:

1. Discussion to bring about the understanding of balance
2. Comparison
3. Statement of problem/teacher demonstration
4. The word base is introduced. Related understanding.

MOTIVATION: Let us do some building today with boxes. Does anybody know how a wall stands up? Would this chair fall if we tried to stand it on two legs? Why? What do you have to do when you stand on one leg (2)?

Boxes are now distributed and the pupils are asked to build so that they will balance.

How will we make the boxes stick? Adhesive is applied to the base of the boxes and they are placed on the support cardboard (3). Make your building go as high as you can.

EVALUATION: How many were able to build their building so that it was very tall? Does your building stand firmly on the support? Who would like to tell me about their building? Did we have to make the part near the ground wider than the top? Why? What do we call the part at the bottom (4)? How many know a building with a wide base?

EXPANDING OPPORTUNITIES: Arranging shapes in a format so as to create a visual balance.

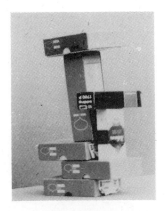 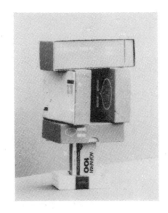

Symetrical and asymetrical balance. Three dimensional.

LEARNING SITUATION: Discovering the relationship of the parts to the whole in a three-dimensional construction

PROCESS: Creating forms from paper bags

MATERIALS: Various sizes of paper bags, brushes, jars, tempera colours, mixing dishes

LEARNING:

1. Recall and Imagination
2. Discussion on characteristics of forms — head, legs, tail etc.
3. Adaptation of available material
4. Teacher demonstration
5. Size and shape comparison

MOTIVATION: How would you like to take a pretend trip to a pet shop and select a pet of your very own? What sort of a pet would you find in a pet shop (1)? — dogs, cats, birds, fish etc. These will be pets we can make ourselves. We can hold them and look at them. Discuss with the children the way the main body and parts are formed. Compare the shapes and sizes of the parts, e.g. is the head as big as the body? How many legs (2)? Is there anything here we could use to start with? (Show box containing paper bags.) Now open out paper bag. How do you think we can make this into different parts of your pet's body (3)? (Newspaper can be torn for stuffing.) Decide what kind of a pet each of you wants to make. (Demonstrate how to tie off different parts of the body with string (4).) Think up ways of tying the different parts. We might twist or wind the string. See if you can make your pet stand up or sit down. When you have your pet finished you may paint it with the colours you like best.

EVALUATION: Tell me about your pet? What important part did you have to think about? How many were able to make their pet stand up? Why did it not stand up? Is he big or small? How big? How small? What sort of skin has he got? How many parts has he got? What part of him is the biggest? Is your pet as big as an elephant (5)? How big is an elephant? Would he be able to come in through the doorway?

EXPANDING OPPORTUNITIES: Making forms in plasticine, e.g. 'A birds' home' with big and small birds.

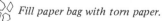 *Fill paper bag with torn paper.*

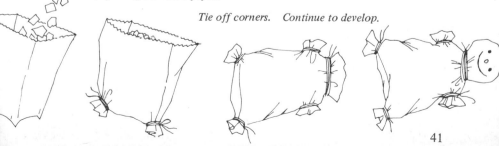

Tie off corners.   Continue to develop.

LEARNING SITUATION: Developing an understanding of tools and media

PROCESS: Painting

MATERIALS: Tempera colour, mixing dishes, jar for water, brushes — large size, cartridge paper

LEARNING:

1. Teacher demonstration
2. Clean brushes are necessary
3. Fully loaded brush, dry brush or little colour in the brush
4. Imagination and association

MOTIVATION: Today we are going to find out all about our paints and how the brush works.

What would happen if you had blue on the brush and you put it into yellow (1)? So we always clean the brush in the water before we put it into a new colour (2)? If we have too much water on the brush what happens? Take up a little clean water on the brush, wipe it on the paper, now dip the brush in colour and touch the water on the paper with the brush (3). Now we will clean out the brush and dip it into a colour and paint it on the paper leaving it wet. If we are going to use another colour what have we do to now? Right, now take up another colour and drop it into the wet colour on your paper, what happened? So now we know what happens when we put wet colour into wet colour. Now we will see what sort of marks you can make with the brush. How many different marks can you make? (A new sheet of paper is distributed.) How would you like to tell a story by putting the marks together, the marks may remind you of something? Use these marks to make a picture (4).

EVALUATION: What did you discover about the paints? What about the brush? How many marks did you find it made? Who found it could make a thin line? What other sort of lines did it make? Tell us about your picture. Did the brush marks turn into something interesting?

EXPANDING OPPORTUNITIES: Discovering how to paint shapes with flat washes of colour.

LEARNING SITUATION: Expressing an idea in colour

PROCESS: Painting

MATERIALS: Tempera colour, brushes, containers for holding colour, jars for water and cartridge paper

LEARNING:

1. Recalling an experience
2. Texture and relationship to shape
3. Imaginative and emotional content of colour
4. The most suitable marks to express texture
5. Relate their inventive creatures with contemporary television creatures

MOTIVATION: How would you like to paint a fierce animal with many legs? Who ever saw a fierce animal (1)? When? How did you feel when you saw it? Where did you see it? Did you feel safe when you saw it?

What colours would you use to show that it is fierce? No doubt you will all use the colour you know is best. The animal you paint is an imaginary animal. Think what his skin will be like (2). What sort of a head will he have? Will you put ears on him? Think what size and shape the animal will be. How big will you make the legs? Don't forget to make him fill the paper. If you have time you may show where he is (background).

EVALUATION: Individual pupils are asked to hold up their paintings and tell about them. Why did you use that colour (3)? What brush marks did you use to show his skin (4)? Who painted wet into wet? Why? How many showed where he lived (background)? Do animals always have to be fierce? Where would you see funny animals and creatures (5)?

EXPANDING OPPORTUNITIES: Painting a fantastic bird.

LEARNING SITUATION: Creating patterns with repetitive shapes

PROCESS: Printing

MATERIALS: Tempera colour, dishes for colour, newsprint (format for printing on), old newspapers for covering desk, printing tool (paper rolled into a ball and one side flattened)

LEARNING:

1. Teacher demonstration   3. Finding relationships
2. Organisation

MOTIVATION: How would you like to print today? What is printing? Is there anything in the room that is printed? Our printing will be a repeat print. Do you remember when we clapped our hand we repeated the line across the page. Today we are going to use a shape and repeat it. (Distribute small pieces of newspaper.) Demonstrate how to crush and press one side flat (1). This is what we are going to print with. We will use this as a printing tool.

Demonstrate how to use the printing tool by dipping it into colour and pressing it on the paper. What do we get when we press the paper printing tool on paper? (A shape.)

Distribute formats and colours and dishes (2).

Press the printing tool into the colour and stamp it on the paper, starting at the top of the sheet of paper. Let it 'walk' across the paper. When we have the first line finished we will repeat another line across the paper until we fill all the space on the paper. Now make a new printing tool and press it into a new colour and stamp it on the empty spaces on your sheet of paper.

EVALUATION: How many were able to fill up the paper with their printing? What do we call this? (A pattern.) Where else can we find a pattern (3)?

EXPANDING OPPORTUNITIES: Pattern making with potato prints.

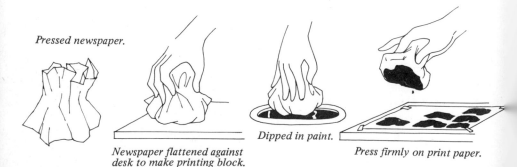

Pressed newspaper.

Newspaper flattened against
desk to make printing block.

Dipped in paint.

Press firmly on print paper.

LEARNING SITUATION: Discovering variation in surface quality

PROCESS: Impressions by rubbings, pasting and arranging

MATERIALS: Crayon, newsprint, leaves, grasses, string, cutting or tearing paper, paste

LEARNING: Impressions — teacher demonstration

1. Identifying the art elements   2. Relating

MOTIVATION: The last day we discovered what shapes were like by painting them. Today we will discover what surfaces are like by taking rubbings of them. (Demonstrate how to take a rubbing by placing a sheet of paper over a surface. With a crayon placed flat on the paper rub the surface using pressure.) Look for shapes that have interesting surfaces, e.g. a variety of leaves, grasses, string etc. Cut the rubbings and paste them down on a new sheet of paper so that they will tell a story.

EVALUATION. What did you find in your rubbings? What was the grass like? When the string folded over what did we get (1)? (Shape) What did we find in the leaves (2)? (Shape and Line) Does the shape and line look like anything you know?

EXPANDING OPPORTUNITIES: Creating new shapes by arranging lines and shapes and taking rubbings of them.

See colour section for surface rubbing.

LEARNING SITUATION: Using flat shapes to express an object

PROCESS: Cutting and arranging paper

MATERIALS: Sheets of assorted coloured paper, paste, paper for support (format) and scissors

LEARNING: Mural – group project

1. Stating the problem   3. Organising and arranging
2. Decoration

MOTIVATION: Let us have a parade (1). How many have seen a parade? Who can tell me about it? What was the parade for? What sort of shapes did you see? (Animals, people, cars, floats, etc.)

Today we are going to make a parade with cut-out shapes in colour paper (2). We will arrange these shapes on a big sheet of paper. Some of us will make the animals and some will make the people and some will make the cars.

When each person has a shape made they will add lines to them to make them look better.

A large sheet of paper is placed on the floor. When each pupil has finished a shape they are asked to place it where they like on the large sheet.

EVALUATION: Pupils are questioned: Does it look like a parade? Why not? (The shapes are too far away from one another.) How should we put them (3)? Where will we put this shape? Are some shapes watching? When everyone agrees on the best arrangement they can paste the shapes down. What do you call it? (A mural.)

EXPANDING OPPORTUNITIES: Making a train shape, joining each carriage.

LEARNING SITUATION: Discovering the difference between regular and irregular shapes

PROCESS: Cutting, tearing and pasting

MATERIALS: Coloured paper, scissors, paste, support (grey sugar paper) 38 x 26cm, different shaped cartons (small size)

LEARNING: Perceiving

1. Class organisation
2. Stating the problem
3. Irregular and regular
4. Teacher demonstration
5. Decoration
6. Organisation on format
7. Background shapes
8. Contrast — large and small
9. Relating shapes to the environment

MOTIVATION: Pupils are asked to collect two different-shaped cartons from the collection box. Look at the different shapes, feel them with your fingers. Try and remember them.

Coloured paper and scissors are now distributed (1). Pupils are now asked to cut the shapes they remember (2). If you cannot remember you may feel the shapes again. Remember we will have some shapes bigger than others. Cartons are now collected and more coloured paper is distributed. Put away carefully the shapes you have cut. Now tear shapes out of the new paper. Make some big and some small.

Question: Is there any difference between the sides of the cut paper and the torn paper (3)? What is the difference? Arrange the shapes on the grey paper. Maybe they will remind you of something. When you know what they are paste them down (paste applied to back of shapes.) (4). Maybe you would like to draw lines on the shapes. What effect would you get by doing this (5)?

EVALUATION: How many were able to fill the grey paper (6)? Did anyone discover that grey shapes are peeping out from between the coloured paper (7)? Did you remember to use big shapes and small shapes (8)? Individual pupils are asked to hold up their arrangements and talk about them. What do they see in them? Does it remind them of anything they have seen (9)?

EXPANDING OPPORTUNITIES: Choosing materials from boxes and arrange them on a support (a texture or a colour arrangement).

LEARNING SITUATION: Creating lines which express movement

PROCESS: Drawing with brush and line

MATERIALS: Tempera colour (one), brushes, containers, jars, paper for protection of the desks and newsprint

LEARNING:

1. Stating the problem
2. Verbalising the movements
3. Relating
4. Creating

MOTIVATION: How many here have played in water? Who can tell me what it was like? Did the water move? How did it move? Did anyone ever throw a stone into the water? How did the water move? Now tell me all about these movements in lines with the brush dipped in paint. Do not forget to fill the sheet of paper with your movements (1).

EVALUATION: Pupils are asked to hold up their drawings and tell about the movements. How many movements did you show (2)? What sort of lines show a splash? When the wind blows the water, what sort of lines represent it? Who can tell me about some other movement of water we have not shown (3) (Waves).

EXPANDING OPPORTUNITIES: Creating pictures to express movement by combining all in a number of different movements.

LEARNING SITUATION: Discovering that hands can smooth clay and make impressions in it

PROCESS: Working with clay or plasticine

MATERIALS: Pottery, clay or plasticine, old newspapers for covering the desks, plastic bags for keeping the clay moist

LEARNING:

1. Procedure
2. Stating the problem
3. Smooth it

4. Flatten it
5. Circle, oval, rectangle
6. Relating

MOTIVATION: Desks are covered with old newspapers for protection. A ball of clay is distributed to each pupil (1). We will find out how the clay is used before we make anything (2). Let us see what happens when we press the clay with our fingers. Who can tell me what happened? When we wipe out the marks, what do we do with the clay (3)? What can we do with the clay when we press it down with our hands (4)? What could we make with flat clay? Maybe dishes. We will make some parts of the dish smooth.

EVALUATION: Let us see now what sort of dishes did you make. Individual pupils are asked to name the shapes of the dishes (5). Would you find any dishes like these at home (6)?

EXPANDING OPPORTUNITIES: Making animals in clay by pulling out the features.

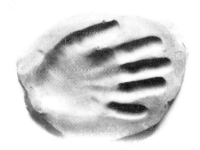

LEARNING SITUATION: To develop the ability to reorganise ideas using dominant and subordinate coloured shapes

PROCESS: Spot, line and shape arrangement

MATERIALS: Construction paper, adhesive, string, buttons, beads, spools etc., scissors

LEARNING: Relating

1. Stating the problem
2. Texture
3. Dominant and subordinate
4. Relating

MOTIVATION: Imagine you are one of Santa's helpers and you are making presents. What sort of presents would you make? (Dolls, toys, etc.) We will make these presents in heavy paper (1) (Construction paper). When you all have thought of the toy or doll you are going to make, cut out the shape on the paper. Now we will put the string on to show the dress (2). Or maybe we will use the string to show the lines on the toy. What will we do with the buttons or the beads (2)?

EVALUATION: Can anyone tell me what was the most important part of the doll or the toy? What was less important? Did anyone use the string to make eyes or the hair or mouth? Have we a word for the less important part (3) (texture)? Did we do something like this before? Can anyone show me the important parts of this room (4)? Are the windows important? What about the floor, is it hard or soft? Is that important? Why?

EXPANDING OPPORTUNITIES: Cutting shapes that are joined and making them stand up. Decorating the shapes with tempera colour.

LEARNING SITUATION: Experimenting with finger painting

PROCESS: Spot painting

MATERIALS: Tempera colour mixed with paste, dishes for paint, jar of water and paper for support (cartridge)

LEARNING: Tools and materials

1. Teacher demonstration
2. Stating the problem
3. Contrast
4. Recall

5. Verbalising and understanding the expressive quality of colour
6. Space
7. Dominance of colour

MOTIVATION: I am sure you would all like to make a painting using dots of colour next to each other. Dip your finger into the colour and then press it on the paper. What happened? (They made a mark or a dot.) Now make a lot of marks (2). Can we make lines with dots or can we make shapes. I hope you will remember to put the dark colour beside the light colour. Why must we do that (3)? What will you tell about? Pupils may choose many subjects, activities and interests from their immediate personal experience (4).

EVALUATION: Now let us see, who would like to tell us about their picture (5)? Why did you use those colours? Why did you like them best? Do we have some parts dark and some parts light? Is there a top and a bottom to your picture (6)? What is the most important part of it? How do we know it is the important part? Is any one colour more important than another (7)?

LEARNING SITUATION: To develop an understanding of space organisation

PROCESS: Drawing

MATERIALS: Black sugar paper and chalk

LEARNING:

1. Space
2. Shape and line combination
3. Organisation within the format
   (teacher demonstration)
4. Space organisation
5. Relation of parts to the whole
6. Relating

MOTIVATION: Tell today about some animal or bird you have seen. What did you see? How big was it? Was it bigger than you? Was it near or far away from you? If it was far away would it be big (1)?

See what happens when we draw with the side of the chalk (2) (the chalk is pushed on the paper held sideways). Now see what happens when we use the point only (line). Now join the shapes and the line to make the animals or birds. Try and fill up the page and put yourself in the picture (3).

EVALUATION: Individual students are questioned. Tell us about your picture. Where are you? Where is the bird? Were you able to make it far from you or near you (4)? How did you make the body (5)? Who made it with chalk held sideways? Was it easier that way? Why? Did anybody use lines to show the feathers or the fur? Was the skin of your animal rough or smooth (6)? Who showed that?

LEARNING SITUATION: Forming with clay to establish an understanding of volume

PROCESS: Modelling

MATERIALS: Clay or plasticine or dough, protection for benches (plastic or old newspapers), sponges for cleaning up

LEARNING:

1. Stating the problem
2. Recalling perceived forms
3. Organisation
4. Grouping forms
5. You can put your hand all around it (it is a volume)

MOTIVATION: Do you remember how we worked the clay (or plasticine) the last day? We were able to press it, slap it. Do you suppose we could form some animal or bird to-day (1)? Perhaps you could tell me about some animal or bird you have seen (2). Benches are protected with plastic or old newspapers. A ball of clay or plasticine is distributed to each pupil (the size of a lemon) (3). First think about what you would like to make, maybe you would enjoy pulling out the different parts; try not to take clay away from your big piece. If little bits fall off, smooth them back with your fingers. When you have formed something to your liking, make it stand and examine it. See if it needs more marks on the surface to tell more about it. If you have time maybe you would like to form some friends for your animal or bird (4).

EVALUATION: Work is placed on display. Show and tell me about your clay form. Tell how you made the marks on the outside. What is the difference between the shape of your animal and the flat shape (5)? Tell what you discovered about pushing and pulling the clay.

EXPANDING OPPORTUNITIES: Pupils may be encouraged to take inspiration from the animal kingdom with such group themes as Noah's Ark, The Zoo, Man and Horse, Family Group, etc.

Modelling with Cornflour

1 cup salt
1½ cup cornflour (cornstarch)
1 cup flour
4 cups water

When water reaches boiling point add salt. Mix flour and cornflour with some cold water; add to boiling water and salt, let this boil until clear. Cool. Knead for a time. Let dry. When ready for use, soften with water. It is possible to reuse this mixture.

Art Growth characteristics

1. Developing control over tools.
2. Using circles for head, eyes, mouth, hands and legs.
3. Exaggeration of parts that are thought important.
4. Draws that which most forcibly impresses him.
5. Beginning to include items of clothing.
6. Use of symbols for objects and humans is developing.
7. Symbols vary in originality and complexity with each child.
8. Usually does not concentrate on any one symbol.
9. Expresses his own ideas and life experience.
10. Beginning to recall detail of facial expression.
11. Beginning to relate symbols to the environment by simple means.
12. Putting together symbols for diverse objects that have relationship in thought.

Behavioural Objectives (intended outcomes for the pupil)

Pupils will be able to:
    Relate the experience of movement to the sheet of paper
    Identify, select and arrange unrelated shapes
    Understand a printing process
    Understand the rhythm of shape
    Recognise hues and their qualities
    Understand weaving process
    Understand the relationship of the tool mark to the expression
    Relate shape to space
    Understand the concept of the three-dimensional form
    Understand unity
    Understand two-dimensional decoration
    Understand how to express facial expressions
    Develop imaginative forms
    Understand contrast of dark and light

Pupils will gain control and manipulate media and tools:
    Paint in tempera colour
    Draw with various tools
    Build and shape
    Relief print
    Print with a stamping tool
    Form with clay
    Assemble forms
    Work with construction card

FIRST CLASS

Learning Situations

1. Lines that continue in a direction.
2. Discovering that line can describe a form.
3. To identify, select and arrange in related shapes.
4. Selecting and arranging rectangular and triangular shapes in a composition.
5. Discovering how to handle tempera paint and seeing what it will do.
6. Discovering lines that are thick and thin.
7. Creating individual units of an idea and arranging them in an area (mural).
8. Using repetition of shape to show rhythm.
9. To experience shapes designed to explain an object two-dimensionally.
10. To develop the ability to reorganise ideas in dominant and subordinate shape.
11. To reorganise ideas in shapes of rich colour.
12. To organise a three-dimensional form from found objects. Enriching surfaces with texture.
13. Developing a source of three-dimensional form.
14. Recognition of (colour) hues and their qualities.
15. To emphasise contour lines of arranged shapes.
16. Discovering how fabric is made and the technique of weaving; creating pattern by weaving lines together.
17. Discovering that different tools make different marks and that these marks may be thought of in relation to a definite idea of expression or experience.
18. To relate shapes to a given size and shape, two-dimensionally.
19. Emphasising the concept of three-dimensional form.
20. Using shapes of colour to create unity and harmony.
21. To enrich a surface area of a two-dimensional form.
22. Discovering facial expressions and expressing them in line.
23. Develping imaginative painting. 'The Fantastic Bird'.
24. To emphasise contrast of dark and light colour.

LEARNING SITUATION: Lines that continue in a direction

PROCESS: Drawing and painting

MATERIALS: Charcoal, crayon, brush, paint

LEARNING: Perceiving

1. Grammar — Line
2. Stating the problem
3. Relating experiences of movement to the sheet of paper
4. Dominant and subordinate
line

MOTIVATION *(Direct Experience)*: Children should be organised to move through the room in such a way that they all move together forming a pathway, all feeling part of the one movement.

Question: What direction should the pathway take through the room? Would it form circles, would it change direction, would part of the pathway intercept another part? Would it continue straight or turn at a sharp angle, would it move in a curve or would it double back on itself? (Recall the directions discovering the movements.) (1).

Show these movements on your paper using crayon, charcoal, brush (2). What are the lines showing us on the paper? (Movement and Direction.) Are these like any other movements that you have experienced (3)? (Walking to school, Traffic.) Show me on a new sheet of paper with line, a journey you have taken. The journey must fill the sheet of paper. In the spaces that you have left over could you show shorter journeys? How would you show the important lines (4)? (Thick and thin, decoration, detail, repetition and contrast.)

EVALUATION: Can you describe the directions in your picture? Did you use all the space? Have you got important lines and lines that are not so important?

EXPANDING OPPORTUNITIES: Further problems, sources, tools that can be used to explore additional lines: Discovering how line can change from thin to thick. Many sources can be found by looking around the room, e.g. legs of the desks, window sashes or frames, lines on children's clothes (fold or patterns).

Lines can describe a form. Look at the many objects in the room, letting the eye travel around the outside of the object (contour line). Tools: Brush, string, crayons, cutting paper lines.

Use contour lines to describe natural forms — animals, birds, insects. Drawing with straws, feathers, twigs, pipe cleaners. Stress filling paper space with lines using individual simple objects rather than complicated ones.

LEARNING SITUATION: Discovering that line can describe a form

PROCESS: Drawing with crayons or any flexible tool

MATERIALS: Paper, any 25 x 38cm smooth finish newsprint or other suitable paper, crayons, ink, tempera colours, felt pens, chalk

LEARNING: Perceiving

1. Grammar — Line
2. Stating the problem
3. Terminology — contour
4. Discovering how the object is made up — its function and making
5. Relating the object to the size of format
6. Change of direction of line
7. Emphasising a continuous line — contour
8. Relating large and small shapes

MOTIVATION *(Visual and Verbal)*: Can you look for an object in the room that we use and tell about it with line (1)? We are going to show on the paper a line that will best tell us about the object (2). What types of lines are there? Could we use a curved line or a straight line to show the object? Can you get your eye to 'walk around' the outside of the object (3)? You could show how your eye walks around the outside of the object (4) with your finger. Can you make the line move the same way as your finger? Can we make our object fill up the page (5)?

EVALUATION: When we look at our drawing has it got curved lines or straight lines? Are the same lines in all the objects? Whereabouts in the object do the curved lines come (6)? How many were able to fill up the page? How many were able to go around the object without stopping (7)? If you stopped can you show me in your drawing where you stopped?

EXPANDING OPPORTUNITIES: Can we now make a picture showing a number of objects in the room and showing how some are big and some are small (8)?

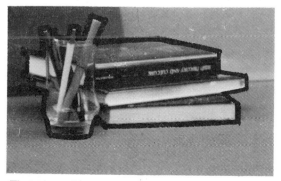

The contour line.

LEARNING SITUATION: To identify, select and arrange unrelated shapes

PROCESS: Cutting shapes from coloured paper, arranging and pasting

LEARNING: Perceiving
(Previous activity: discovering that geometrical shapes can be identified with shapes, objects in the environment. Present acitivity: discovering the identity of shapes as things in themselves.)

1. Asking the children to imagine   3. Stating the problem
   possible combinations of
   shapes, hybrid shapes
2. Overlapping

MOTIVATION *(Visual and Verbal)*: Ask the pupils to think of an object or animal they have seen. What sort of a shape does it have? Could you cut out this shape on a piece of paper? Now think of another object or animal that has a completely different shape and cut it out of your piece of coloured paper. Discuss the differences. Some are straight, some are curved. What sort of shape would you get if you combined these two different shapes together (1)?

Place both shapes together on your piece of support paper so that one covers (2) the other in some places (3). Have you now got a new shape? Do you think you could find other shapes by moving the shapes around more? When you discover a shape that you are happy with, paste it down. From the remaining paper, ask the pupils to cut out several different shapes that contrast the original one hybrid shape. Ask the children to think about the size of these shapes on the sheet of paper. Some shapes can be hidden by others. Don't forget to place some of these shapes near the edge of your sheet of paper.

EVALUATION: Ask the children to examine their arrangements to see if they can find new shapes that are hidden between the pasted down shapes.

EXPANDING OPPORTUNITIES: Discovering positive and negative shapes.

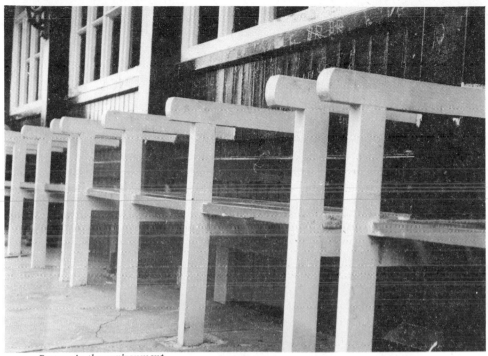

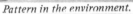

Pattern in the environment.

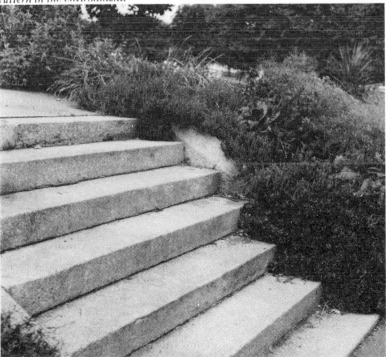

LEARNING SITUATION: Selecting and arranging rectangular and triangular shapes in composition

PROCESS: Cutting shapes from coloured paper, arranging and pasting

MATERIALS: Sheets of assorted coloured paper, white paper for a support, scissors, adhesive

LEARNING: Perceiving

1. Visual recall
2. Stating the problem
3. Arrangement of shapes within the (rectangle) sheet of paper
4. Visual recall

MOTIVATION *(Visual and Verbal)*: Help children to identify rectangular and triangular shapes with shapes in their immediate environment, e.g. buildings, cars, boxes, etc. What way are these shapes normally arranged? Do you find them on their own or are they usually grouped together? Where do you see these groupings (1)? Location of groupings are discussed and amplified, e.g. houses in the street, cars in the car park. Are these shapes all the same size or do we find they have different sizes? Are some of these shapes nearer or do some appear further away?

We will now cut large and small rectangles, also large and small triangles, and arrange these on your paper so that they form groups (2). Don't forget to put the triangular shapes with the rectangular shapes so that you get interesting groupings. Think of some of the things you see every day, and see how they could be used in your arrangement.

EVALUATION: Ask the pupils to focus on the grouping they have arranged and to talk about them (3). Discuss geometrical forms in the environment (4).

EXPANDING OPPORTUNITIES: Discover that shapes can be enriched and given meaning with line, e.g. windows, doors, brickwork, and other linear treatment developed from the pupils' visual recall.

LEARNING SITUATION: Discovering how to handle tempera paint and seeing what it will do

PROCESS: Painting

MATERIALS: Brushes size 8, premixed tempera — red, blue, yellow, green, orange, black and white, cartridge paper 25 x 38cm

LEARNING: Media exploration

1. Teacher demonstration
2. Flat wash (Art vocabulary)
3. Dominate and subordinate
4. Details, features, decoration
5. Handling of media

MOTIVATION: Today we are going to see if we can make the paint lie flat on the paper. Where can we find colour that is painted flat? What do we mean when we say it is flat? (The painted wall or woodwork.)

Could we make the paint flat if we had put a little paint on the brush? We must take a lot of paint on the brush and rub it across the top part of the shape. If the brush goes dry we must load it up again. This time we move it across the shape touching the last stroke which will be still wet (1).

Paper is distributed. Pupils are asked to fill in big shapes with flat colour (2) as an experiment.

When flat wash is completed more paper is distributed. Pupils are now asked to paint large figures. What will the figure be? Maybe we would like to paint a postman or a milkman or a butcher or a soldier or a jockey or an air hostess. What is the important part in all these figures? The uniform; the biggest part of colour. We won't forget to show the important part with flat colour. What are the parts that are not so important (3)? We won't forget to make these flat too. When we have all the flat parts painted and dry we might like to paint lines on them, what are the lines for (4)?

EVALUATION: Let us see now who was able to paint in all the shapes flat (5). Individual paintings are held up. Why do we know it is the postman, etc. Do we know people by the clothes they wear? What else do clothes tell us?

EXPANDING OPPORTUNITIES: Dominant and subordinate shapes — a street picture.

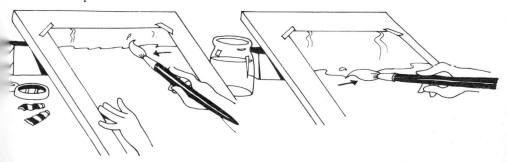

LEARNING SITUATION: Discovering lines that are thick and thin

PROCESS: Cutting, arranging, pasting

MATERIALS: Dark and light coloured paper (black and white if available), cold water paste, jar and brush for applying paste, scissors, bag for waste paper, paper to cover desk

LEARNING:

1. Using art elements to develop pupil observation
2. Teacher demonstration
3. Statement of problem
4. Integrative
5. Teacher demonstration
6. Art vocabulary
7. Relating lines to reading
8. Graphic symbols, movements, left to right, spacing etc.

MOTIVATION: How many are able to show me thick and thin lines in the room (1)? We are going to use thick and thin lines cut out of paper today. Distribute dark paper. Demonstrate how to fold paper into strips (all thick, all thin). Demonstrate how to cut the folded paper with the scissors (2). When sufficient thick and thin strips are cut, ask the pupils to arrange these lines to show a particular movement (3). (This may be a recalled movement that was experienced in PE class) (4).

Demonstrate how to paste strips by laying them flat on the desk and pasting them down. (Desks should be covered with paper.)

EVALUATION: What do these strips of paper remind you of? (Lines.) What sort of lines (6)? (Thick and thin lines.) How many were able to fill up the paper with the thick and thin lines? Does your painting show movement? Tell us about the movement. What other type of movement can we tell about with line? Do we find thick and thin lines in letters in our books (7)? Do they move too (8)? How do they move?

EXPANDING OPPORTUNITIES: Lines that move into shapes and show movement.

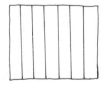

Rule off wide strips.

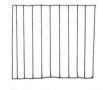

Rule off narrow strips.

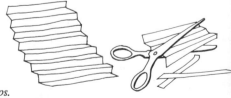

Fold on lines backwards and forwards.   *Cut strips.*

LEARNING SITUATION: Creating individual units of an idea and arranging them in an area (mural)

PROCESS: Painting shapes and arranging them

MATERIALS: One large sheet of cartridge paper, paints, scissors, paste

LEARNING:

1. Stating the problem
2. Verbal motivation
3. Arrangement of shapes
4. Satisfactory grouping
5. Mural

MOTIVATION: Today we will all help to make a big wall picture (mural) (1). First we will 'think out' what the picture will be about. Discuss some group activity such as playing games (2). When pupils decide on the games, they group themselves as the players. When you think what part you will play in the game, draw yourself on your own piece of paper. Don't forget to make yourself big. When you are finished, cut the figure out and pin it to the big sheet of paper. We will need people to draw things to show where the games are taking place. You will also cut these out and pin them to the big sheet of paper.

EVALUATION: We will all look and decide if all the shapes are in the right place (3). Should we group the shapes? Why? What way should we group them? Should we put important parts together. When we are all satisfied that everything is in its right place (4), we will paste the parts down. How do we think out a picture? Who knows what this sort of picture is called (5)? Where else would you see murals? (Public buildings.)

EXPANDING OPPORTUNITIES: Pupils may select other subjects for murals 'Street Scenes', 'A Journey', 'Musicians'.

LEARNING SITUATION: Using repetition of shape to show rhythm

PROCESS: Stamping, printing with a potato

MATERIALS: Plastic knives, potatoes, tempera colour, dishes for holding paint, newsprint, old newspaper for covering desks

LEARNING:

1. Teacher demonstration
2. Procedure and class organisation
3. Stating the problem
4. Relating delph, pottery, buildings. (Repeat pattern.)

MOTIVATION: We are going to make a printing tool today. Would anybody like to tell what printing is? Our printing tool will be made from a potato. Shapes are cut in the halved potato, dipped into colour and stamped on the sheet of paper (1). Desks are covered with old newspaper. Potatoes are distributed and pupils are asked to cut shapes. The waste potato is then put into a container. Now paint and paper can be distributed (2). Pupils are asked to stamp the printing tool across the top of the paper in a row and then a second row until they fill up the sheet of paper (3).

EVALUATION: Show me who was able to fill up the paper with print. Can you find background shapes? What were you doing when you were stamping the tool? (Repeating a shape.) (4) Where else would you find repeated printed shapes?

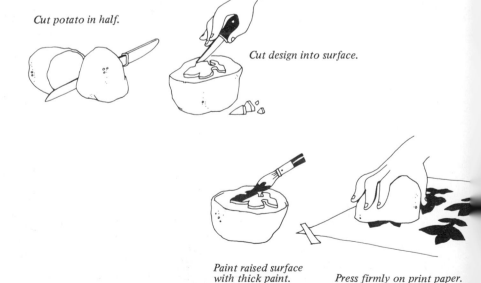

Cut potato in half.

Cut design into surface.

Paint raised surface with thick paint.   *Press firmly on print paper.*

LEARNING SITUATION: To experience shapes designed to explain an object two-dimensionally

PROCESS: Arrangement of cut-out shapes, mounting and arranging selected pieces in a frieze

MATERIALS: Assorted coloured paper, strings, adhesive, scissors, cartridge paper for support (format), 25 x 38cm.

LEARNING: Visual movement as decoration

1. Stating the problem

2. Frieze, decoration, pottery, borders

MOTIVATION: How would you like to make a picture that fills one whole wall of the room? This will be made of paper cut-outs or you may tear shapes. We will make our picture tell of some fantastic machine that moves We will each add a piece to it. What parts of this machine move? There are big parts and small parts. Can you name them? Wheels, legs, pistons, belts, spokes. We will have to think of these as shapes and arrange them on the sheet of paper you have (format) (1). Cartridge paper has already been distributed. Maybe you would like to tell more about the shapes by adding lines. You can stick down string or thread to show the lines. When the pupils have their formats completed, they are asked to arrange them in a frieze across the wall.

EVALUATION: Have we arranged them well? Does it show movement? Is it making our eyes move from one end of the wall to the other? Do we move, or does it? Can anyone tell me where they would find a similar picture that leads our eye around an object (2)?

EXPANDING OPPORTUNITIES: Cut-outs may be made from drawings, different kinds of paper, buttons, beads, matches, etc., may be added, designs may be in groups or single mountings.

LEARNING SITUATION: To develop the ability to reorganise ideas in dominant and subordinate shape

PROCESS: Using any flexible tool which will help to express an idea

MATERIALS: Cartridge paper or sugar paper, tempera paint, felt or sponge, straws, fingers or cardboard

LEARNING:

1. Dominant
2. Subordinate
3. Stating the problem

4. Organisation of space
5. Background shape emphasised
6. Overlapping

MOTIVATION: What game do you like playing best? Can you tell me about the things that are important or big (1) in it? What about the things that are not important, we could call these the helping things (2). We can 'tuck in' (overlap) the helping things. We will make the important parts big. Make a picture of your game (3). We will make the picture go away up to the top of the paper and down to the bottom if possible (4). Be sure all parts of the paper help to tell the story of the game (5).

EVALUATION: How would we know the most important thing in your picture? Do you have 'helper parts'? Are there any tuck-in parts (6)? When we use tuck-in parts what happens (4)? Are there things in the air space in your picture?

EXPANDING OPPORTUNITIES: Children may choose many subjects, activities and interests from personal experiences. How I eat my meals, visiting the dentist. They may draw in a variety of media.

LEARNING SITUATION: To reorganise ideas in shapes of rich colour

PROCESS: Painting with tempera

MATERIALS: Environment, tempera paint, newsprint, large brushes, cleaning-up materials

LEARNING:

1. Geometrical shapes
2. Rectangles of different sizes
   – triangles
3. Stating problem – dominant
   – subordinate
4. Relating shape to the format, overlapping
5. Combination of two art elements

MOTIVATION: Can you tell something important about where you live or the street you like best? Are all the houses the same shape (1)? Would some buildings have other shapes as well as rectangles (2)? Could we think of boxes with triangles on top? How would you describe a church? Do you see anything in the room with the same shape? Show on your paper the important buildings (3). The big ones and small ones. What are the small shapes? Windows, doors, chimneys. You might like to show people outside the buildings. What clothes will they wear? Spread the story all over the paper (4). Maybe some shapes will be tucked-in (5).

EVALUATION: Individual pupils are asked to hold up their pictures and are questioned. Have you got different houses? Did anybody think of making some of the houses dark in colour? How many used lines as well as shapes (5)? Who has things that touch the top edge of the paper, the bottom edge and sides?

EXPANDING OPPORTUNITIES: Further sources for subject matter, ideas and subsequent paintings could be: the pet shop; grocery shop; supermarket; the drapery shop; restaurant; park; the churchyard; the fire station; the fair green.

LEARNING SITUATION: To organise a three-dimensional form from found objects. Enriching surfaces with textures

PROCESS: Construction and decoration

MATERIALS: Found objects, discarded materials of all kinds such as buttons, beads, spools, paper, small cartons, boxes, fabrics, tubes, string, yarn, rope. Tools to include scissors, pins, paper fasteners, adhesive

LEARNING:

1. Stating the problem
2. Cylindrical
3. Figure
4. Eyes, nose, mouth, hair
5. Arranging and organising
6. Extending imagination
7. Relating

MOTIVATION: How would you like to make a fantastic figure from tubes or boxes. We will all think about the figure. Individual students are questioned about what figure they intend to make. We will have to join the head, arms, hands, legs and feet (1). How will we make these? Maybe we could cut the tube for the neck (2). Why would we use the tube for the neck? What else could we use tubes for? What would you use for the body (3)? Discuss ways of joining and adding. When we have the important part finished, what will we do? We will paint in the detail (4). What is the detail? Maybe we could design clothes. We could make them from the cloths we have in the collection box. What would we use the beads and buttons for? (Eyes.) Do not forget to use the string to decorate the clothes (5).

EVALUATION: How many can get their figure to stand up? Maybe there are some you have to hold? Individual pupils are asked to tell about their fantastic figure (6). Discuss what was used to enhance the surface. Where else would you find a surface that was decorated (7)? How does decoration change the surface?

EXPANDING OPPORTUNITIES: Various size bags can be painted and decorated with paper, yarn and tempera colour. The bags can be stuffed, painted and mounted on lolly-pop sticks.

LEARNING SITUATION: Developing a source of three-dimensional form

PROCESS: Modelling

MATERIALS: Sawdust, adhesive (cold water paste) or plasticine or clay or paper pulp. Tools: fingers

LEARNING: Expressing three dimensions

1. Teacher demonstration
2. Stating the problem

3. Emphasis on scale of parts

MOTIVATION: Can you find an object in the room that is not flat? How do we know it is not flat? Teacher shows a ball of sawdust, papier mache, plasticine or clay to the class.

Question: How can we change this round ball (1)? (Jabbing, pinching, pressing, adding.) Can we make it stand? See if you can make something interesting that will stand (2).

EVALUATION: How many were able to make it stand? Individual pupils are asked to tell about what they made and how they made it. They may be questioned on the relationship of the parts to the whole of the form (3).

EXPANDING OPPORTUNITIES: Painting the form and decorating

Use assorted oddments. First Class No. 12.

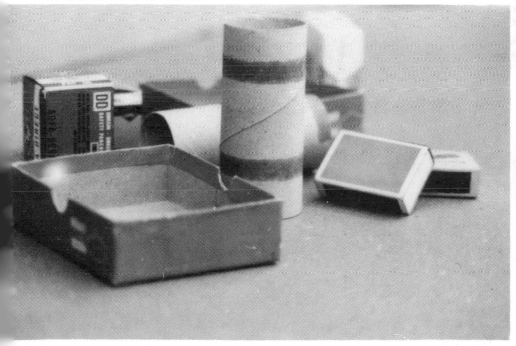

LEARNING SITUATION: Recognition of hues (colour) and their qualities

PROCESS: Painting with coloured shapes

MATERIALS: Old magazines (coloured pages), adhesive (cold water paste), paper for support (format)

LEARNING:

1. Stating the problem
2. Chroma and intensities organisation
3. A recalled experience
4. Dominance

MOTIVATION: Old magazines are distributed to each pupil. Who can find colours that are of the same family (1)? What do we mean when we say they are of the same family? The red family are all the same but different (2). Make bundles of each colour family.

The support paper is distributed and a spoon of paste placed on a folded glossy surface page (as a support for paste) to each pupil. Tell a story now by adding the coloured pieces. Pupils may supply their own story.

Questions: What are you going to tell about (3)? What colours will you use for it? What colour family will you make important (4)?

EVALUATION: Are some colours warm? What would the opposite be? (Cold.) Who used a colour family that was warm? Why? How many used dark colour beside light colours? Why? Did we make sure to fill up the page with the story? Did anyone think of the background?

EXPANDING OPPORTUNITIES: Topics that could be treated include 'Cold air passing into a warm room', 'Crowd scene, one side pushing the other', 'A traffic jam'.

LEARNING SITUATION: To emphasise contour lines of arranged shapes

PROCESS: Rubbing prints

MATERIALS: Construction paper (heavy card), newsprint, cartridge paper for support (format), scissors, crayons

LEARNING:

1. Stating the problem
2. Teacher demonstration
3. Positive and negative shapes
4. Emphasising contour lines

MOTIVATION: How would you like to make a picture by a rubbing print (1)? Shapes are cut from the construction paper and are arranged on the format (cartridge paper) (2). When we are arranging the shapes what must we do? Let some shapes touch the edge of the format. We might find new shapes in the background (3). When we are satisfied with the arrangement we will place and paste them down. Now we will make a rubbing. How will we do that? Place newsprint flat over shapes and with the crayon held sideways, rub the surface (2).

EVALUATION: What do we call the lines that appeared on the paper? (Contour lines) (4). What made the best rubbing? Did we find new shapes in the background?

EXPANDING OPPORTUNITIES: Collecting different surface rubbings and cutting shapes out of them, then arranging them on a support and pasting.

See colour section for example.

LEARNING SITUATION: Discovering how fabric is made, and the technique of weaving; creating pattern by weaving lines together

PROCESS: Weaving

MATERIALS: Cartridge paper for loom, sheets of coloured paper

LEARNING:

1. Weave or weaving on a loom   2. Teaching demonstration
(weft and warp)

MOTIVATION: We will all look at a piece of fabric. See how you can pull it in different ways. How does it feel? See if you can draw out some threads. Discover how the horizontal and vertical are caught together (1). How would you like to weave? Instead of thread we will use paper strips. This is how we will do it. (Discuss loom.)

Sheet of cartridge is distributed to each pupil. Fold this paper in half. Rule one inch margin on the short and long sides but not on the folded side. Cut lines one inch apart from the fold to the margin. Open out and we have a set of horizontal strips held in position by a margin. This is a paper loom. These strips are called 'warp'. Now we will cut another sheet of paper (different colour) into one inch strips. We will cut them all the way out this time. These are called the 'weft' strips. Weft strips are woven into the warp – one under, one over – every second strip to alternate until the loom is filled.

EVALUATION: Examination and discussion of finished mats. Who got the colour to change? Who got all one colour? Who made stripes? Who got a good finish on the edge?

EXPANDING OPPORTUNITIES: Experimenting with different colours. Using different textures of paper. Painting designs on the strips before and after weaving. Varying the widths of the strips.

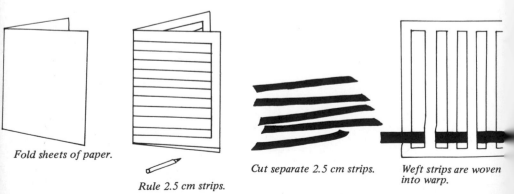

Fold sheets of paper.

Rule 2.5 cm strips.

Cut separate 2.5 cm strips.

Weft strips are woven into warp.

LEARNING SITUATION: Discovering that different tools make different marks and these marks may be thought of in relation to a definite idea of expression or experience

PROCESS: Painting

MATERIALS: Liquid tempera, newsprint, sticks, brushes, rope, feathers, rags, sponges, cardboard, strips, drinking-straws

LEARNING:

1. Stating the problem

MOTIVATION: When we were painting before, what tools did we use to put the paint on the surface of the paper? (Brushes, fingers.) Were they hard or soft? Today we are going to find the marks these tools make (Tools are shown to pupils) (1).

Try and select a hard tool and a soft tool. Find out what marks the tool makes on the sheet of paper. You may find by holding it in different ways you get different marks. What tool would give the softness of fur, which one the roughness of rock? Which one gives us lines? Which one gives us shapes?

Distribute a new sheet of paper to each pupil. On the new sheet of paper put the marks together to make a picture. Maybe the marks remind you of something, e.g. trees, rocks, sky, clouds, etc.

EVALUATION: What did we find out about the tool? Individual pupils hold up their painting. Questions (to stimulate flexibility in the use of tools): What tool did you find best to paint things that are rough? What tool was best for things that are soft? What is best for making line? What did you find was best for shape? Is it important how you hold the tool? Tell me about it.

EXPANDING OPPORTUNITIES: Discover new ways to use a soft pencil.

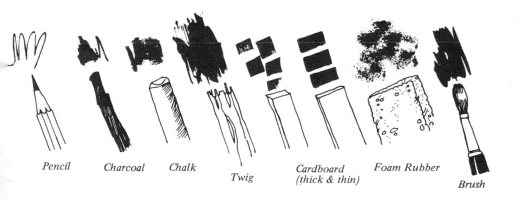

Pencil　　*Charcoal*　　*Chalk*　　*Twig*　　*Cardboard (thick & thin)*　　*Foam Rubber*　　*Brush*

LEARNING SITUATION: To relate shapes to a given size and shape, two-dimensionally

PROCESS: Cutting shapes, painting, pasting

MATERIALS: Two sheets of newsprint 25 x 38cm, paste, tempera, scissors, brushes

LEARNING:

1. Relationship   2. Stating the problem

MOTIVATION: We will think of size today. The questioning approach may be utilised. Who can name a large animal? How large is he? Is he larger than yourself? Is he larger than a man? Is a fly large? Why? If you put the fly in a match box how large would he be? What are we thinking about? We are thinking about relating sizes (1). We will all now think of a shape of a large animal and relate it to the four sides of the paper. Maybe you would like to put more shapes in the background related to the animal. Maybe your animal will be bigger than a man. Will the house be bigger than the man? Cut the shape of the animal out of one sheet of paper. Think of the size it has to fit into on the other sheet of paper. When you are satisfied, paste it down. Now with your brush and paint draw shapes in the background.

EVALUATION: Who would like to tell us about their picture? What size is your animal's tail? Did you make him in relation to the sheet of paper? If your animal was in this room how big would he be? Further questions may be asked to strengthen their concepts of relationship of size.

EXPANDING OPPORTUNITIES: Creating dioramas (shape placed in a box leaving the front side open).

LEARNING SITUATION: Emphasising the concept of three-dimensional form

PROCESS: Construction, cutting and fastening papers of various colours

MATERIALS: Construction paper, assorted coloured papers 25 x 38cms, scissors

LEARNING:

1. Comparison   2. Teacher demonstration

MOTIVATION: Who knows what three-dimensional means? Are there three-dimensional things in this room? Here is a clue. I can see something high and it is wide and you can walk around it. (Chair.) Why do we say three-dimensional (1)? Because it has thickness. Who can show me something else that is three-dimensional? Let us make figures today that are three-dimensional. How could we make this paper look three-dimensional? (By rolling it into a cylinder or folding it into a rectangular form or overlapping into a cone) (2). What part of the body would we use the roll for? (Torso, legs, arms.) Would we require different thicknesses for the arms and legs? What will we make for the head? (Cube.) When we have all the parts made we will join them with adhesive tape.

EVALUATION: Individual pupils are asked to explain about the construction: Is the head related to the body? What about the arms, are they long enough? Are you satisfied with the legs?

EXPANDING OPPORTUNITIES: Costumes may be created and painted.

LEARNING SITUATION: Using shapes of colour to create unity and harmony

PROCESS: Arranging transparent shapes of colour

MATERIALS: Tissue paper, black sugar paper, paste, pencils, felt markers, scissors

LEARNING:

1. Teacher demonstration
2. Stating the problem
3. Large and small
4. The yellow family, the blue family

MOTIVATION: Would you like to design a 'see-through' picture of interesting colours today? What happens when we cover a colour with the same colour? (It darkens) (1). See what happens when we have two different colours. (They change.) Black paper is distributed (2). We will cut shapes in the black paper making sure they are related (3). (Remember when we made the related shapes.) We will cover this shape with coloured tissue paper. We will use related colour, all warm colours, all cold colours (4). When you are satisfied with your related colour paste them down. (Paste applied to black paper and tissue paper pressed down.)

EVALUATION: How many of you carefully selected your colour families? Were you able to make the colours darker? Did you make new colours by mixing two colours? Would you like to tell about your design?

EXPANDING OPPORTUNITIES: Drawings may be made with crayons on muslin and then ironed on the wrong side with a hot iron. These can be used as wall hangings.

LEARNING SITUATION: To enrich a surface area of a two-dimensional form

PROCESS: Cutting and decorating

MATERIALS: Large sheets of soft card, tempera paint, string, brushes, scissors, staples

MOTIVATION: We will pretend we are costume designers for our play. (Integrating with drama.) We will work in teams (2 or 4 children). A hole is cut in the centre of the large sheet of paper, placed over the head and caught at the side by strings passed through punched holes. Other pieces may be attached with a stapler (For fringe or hem). Now we will think of the centre part. (Discuss kinds of designs such as border, strips, plaids, flowers.)

EVALUATION: What kind of colour do you like to see in costumes? Explain how you designed your costume and tell why you picked that design.

EXPANDING OPPORTUNITIES: Open weave such as onion sacks may be interwoven with paper strips, twigs, straw, plastic strips to create fantastic costumes.

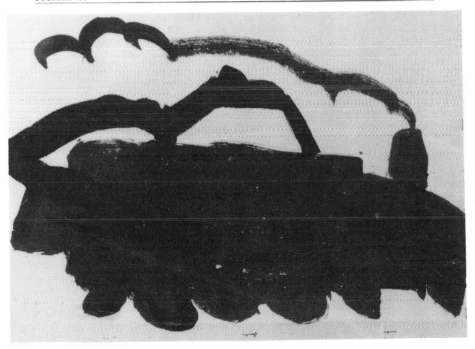

A steam engine. Age: 5. Idea and Concept.

LEARNING SITUATION: Discovering facial expressions and expressing them in line

PROCESS: Cutting and painting

MATERIALS: Construction card, tempera paint, scissors, brushes, string, puncher

MOTIVATION: How would you like to make masks today? When do we wear masks? Who also wore masks? (Africans, American Indians, Greek actors.) What are they for? What expression do they show? (Fierce, sad, happy, sly, mean, etc.) We will remember all these expressions now.

Card is distributed. A large egg shape is drawn on it. Now think what expression your mask will have. What lines will you use, also what colours? Paint in the lines and colours when you are satisfied. When finished you may cut holes for the eyes and mouth and punch a hole on each side for the string.

EVALUATION: Who made a happy expression? Who sad, who fierce, etc.? How could you make it fiercer, sadder, etc.?

EXPANDING OPPORTUNITIES: Drawing figures to express feeling.

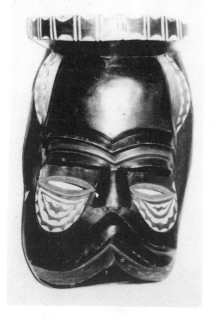
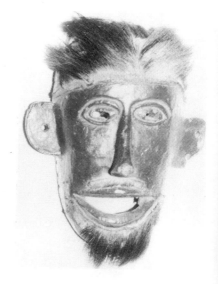

Masks. African.

LEARNING SITUATION: Developing imaginative painting, 'The Fantastic Bird'

PROCESS: Painting

MATERIALS: Tempera paint, newsprint 25 x 38cm approx., brushes — school fitch size 8, mixing dishes, containers for colours and newspaper for protecting the desks.

LEARNING:

1. Stating the problem   3. Organisation
2. Recalling

MOTIVATION: I am sure you would all like to paint a fantastic bird (1). I am sure you all know something about birds. How do they move? (Fly.) What shape is the body of the bird? Are they all the same size? What are the legs (2) like? Are they jointed? What is the birds mouth like? Do they have different sized beaks? What about the feathers, are they all the same colour? What do birds eat (2)?

Our fantastic bird will have strange coloured feathers, a beak you would never see, funny legs, strange eyes. Instead of eating worms we will have him doing something else.

Desks are covered, materials, paper and dishes, are distributed (3). Make sure you fill the paper with your bird. You might also think of important lines.

EVALUATION: Individual pupils are asked to talk about their fantastic birds: Why did you use that colour? Did you fill the paper? Do artists paint fantastic birds or make things with birds shapes?

EXPANDING OPPORTUNITIES: Painting a fantastic horse.

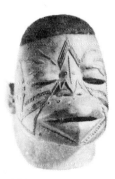

African.

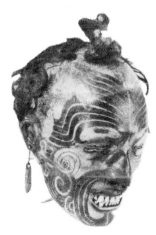

Maori.

LEARNING SITUATION: To emphasise contrast of dark and light colour

PROCESS: Tearing and pasting

MATERIALS: Grey paper for support 25 x 38cm, black sugar paper, newsprint, paste, printed pages from magazines

LEARNING: Expressing dark and light

1. Contrast
2. Stating the process
3. Teacher demonstration
4. Stating the problem
5. Emphasising contrast

MOTIVATION: How would you like to make a picture with black and white paper? When we put black paper beside white paper what do we make (1)? (A contrast.) Why do we not put black beside black? (No contrast.) Black and white paper is distributed, pupils are asked to tear the paper into small shapes (2) and make a bundle of black and a bundle of white. The grey paper is now distributed (support). The pages from the magazines are distributed and the pupils are asked to fold the pages in half. A spoon of paste is now placed on the folded page. The technique of buttering on the small shapes is explained (3). We will let all the small shapes tell a story (4). What story would you like to tell? Individual pupils are questioned to help them to clarify their ideas.

EVALUATION: Individual pupils are asked to hold up their pictures and tell about them: Why did we use the grey paper? What would happen if we used black paper (5)? How many made black lines by adding small pieces of black together?

EXPANDING OPPORTUNITIES: Creating hybrid shapes by adding two or more different shapes together (geometrical).

Art Growth Characteristics

1. Beginning to organise the meaningful forms and shapes as he sees himself as part of his environment.
2. Drawing the 'Base Line' as an indication of floor or ground.
3. Several happenings or steps in a time sequence may occur in one picture.
4. May draw 'X-Ray' pictures, showing the inside and the outside of a house or room.
5. Has ability to relate colour to object.
6. Beginning to develop a knowledge of joints and how to make bodies move and bend.
7. A strong desire to express himself with clarity.
8. Symbols that have emotional or intellectual importance may be made larger than others related to it.
9. Colour is often chosen for emotional appeal rather than for resemblance to the natural object.
10. Sky is becoming blue and grass green.
11. Very inventive, vivid imagination.
12. Tends to use reason in solving problems.

Behavioural Objectives (intended outcomes for the pupil)

The pupil will be able to:
Describe movement through line
Describe distance
Relate shape to area
Relate unrelated forms
Understand the balance of dark and light
Understand unity
Understand hues and their qualities
Understand formal and informal balance
Understand pattern
Express emotions and feeling through line
Understand symbolic shapes
Express the actions of the human figure
Understand tone value

The pupil will gain control and manipulate media and tools:
Discover the technique of tempera painting
Potato printing
Drawing
Modelling
Weaving with paper
Taking rubbing prints
Cutting and construction in paper
Arranging shape in a format

81

Learning Situations

1. Discovering lines that describe movement.
2. Discovering how lines that are grouped together according to their direction and position can create distance.
3. Discovering that changing levels can create distance.
4. Relating different sizes to different areas.
5. Discovering how to relate unrelated forms.
6. To express an idea through modified colour contrasts of warm to cool.
7. To show balance dependent on dark and light contrast.
8. To emphasise contrast of line.
9. Designing in construction card, shapes to express an idea.
10. To unify a design by using harmonising shapes of colour and light.
11. To organise simple lines and shapes in space expressing a personal experience.
12. Discovering that colour, an element of art, has a wide range of hue and tone.
13. Understanding the principle of balance, formal and informal.
14. Building a bowl by using the pinch clay method emphasising symmetry.
15. To develop pattern by the repetition of shape and colour.
16. Selecting and arranging two-dimensional shape to creating a pattern for a relief print.
17. To create a three-dimensional form establishing unity of colour and texture.
18. To describe form in line and contrasting imaginative colour.
19. To express emotions through line.
20. To organise symbolic shapes in a composition.
21. To organise figure shapes to express action.
22. Developing an understanding of linear treatment of a subject.
23. Grouping various geometric shapes to create a subject matter.
24. Discovering space and expressing a form in space (Expressing space on a flat surface).

Movement (photo Szelinski. Source Archives 2238).

LEARNING SITUATION: Discovering lines that describe movement

PROCESS: Drawing

MATERIALS: Pencil, crayon, chalk, board, etc., white paper as support

LEARNING: Perceiving

1. Looking at environment
2. Stating the problem
3. Use large sheets of paper
4. Contour
5. Recreating linear shapes with movement
6. Movement of the contour line
7. Related and unrelated lines

MOTIVATION: *(Verbal and Visual)*: Could you imagine yourself moving? Are you in something, e.g. a car, bus or are you walking or running? How did you move? Did you change direction? Can you think of some activity to do in which there might be different movements, e.g. up/down, left/right, swinging, climbing, crawling, etc? All of these things which you do, perhaps a lot, have movement. Now let us look for something unusual that has movement, e.g. an insect, a shell, fish in a bowl, birds flying, trees moving in the wind, butterflies, etc. (1).

When you have found something, show how it moves with a line (2). What can you now do with this line? Let it make the same movements on the sheet of paper so that it makes a big shape (3, 4). What does this 'shape' suggest to you? Could it be made into something? Take more movements and add them to what you have on your piece of paper (5).

EVALUATION: What movement does your shape show? Is the movement inside your shape or outside it (6)? Do the different lines look well together? Are they friendly or unfriendly?

EXPANDING OPPORTUNITIES: Creating shapes that express movement.

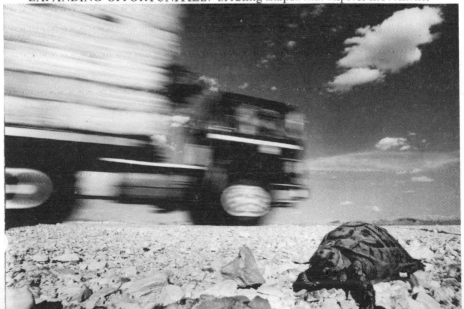

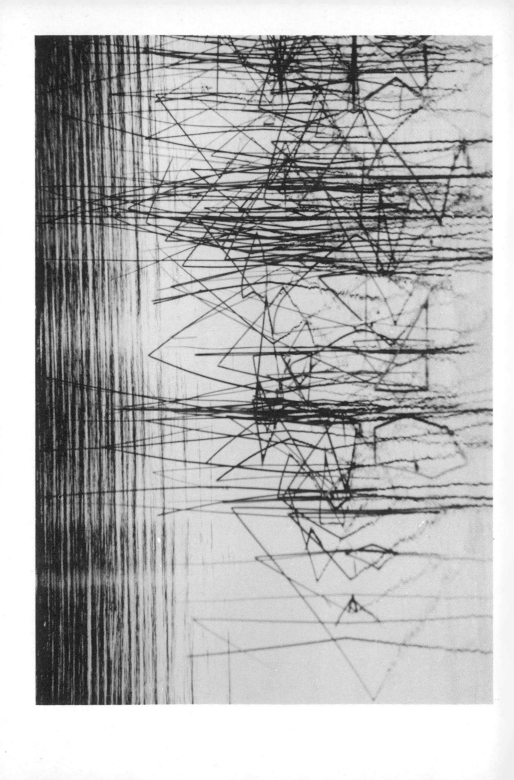

LEARNING SITUATION: Discovering how lines that are grouped together according to their direction and position can create distance

PROCESS: Painting with cardboard strips

MATERIALS: Newsprint, cardboard, flat trays to hold paint (biscuit tin tops), tempera paints, strips of cardboard cut in different lengths and widths (short and long), or sticks

LEARNING: Perceiving

1. Vertical, horizontal, oblique, receding
2. Stating the problem
3. Demonstrate how to use the cardboard strips
4. Directions, e.g. vertical, horizontal, oblique, etc.
5. Position, up/down, middle, left/right, front/back, etc.
6. Focal point
7. Nearness and distance
8. Receding lines

MOTIVATION *(Verbal and Visual)*: There are many types of line in this room, many going in different directions. Would you like to look and discover for yourselves how many different directions there are? Can you name the directions (1)?

We will draw these lines now and discover what happens on the sheet of paper (2). Before we start we must see how many of these lines go together. Are there short lines together? Are there long lines together?

Decide whether you wish to use the short side or the long side of the cardboard. Dip it in the paint and press it down on the paper (3). When pressing the tool on the paper, remember to place it in the direction of the lines you are looking at (4). Think of where you are going to place these directions on your piece of paper (5). Do the lines you have made with the tools move on your sheet of paper from the top to the bottom? Do they move from left to right, or are some in front and some behind? Do any rest in the middle? Do some of these lines go to the edge of your paper? Do the lines appear near or far away (7)? What would we call these lines (8)?

EVALUATION: Will you put all the lines that are vertical together? Will you put all the lines that are horizontal together? Will you put the lines that are going away from you together?

EXPANDING OPPORTUNITIES: Could you now imagine yourself as worms? Draw the things in the room the way you think a worm would see them, showing the things that are near and the things that are far away.

Opposite: Line in the environment.

LEARNING SITUATION: Discovering that changing levels can create distance

PROCESS: Drawing with chalk, crayon, pencil, felt pens, etc.

MATERIALS: Any suitable paper for a support

LEARNING: Perceiving
(Previous activity — relating size to format; present activity — horizontal positioning used to express distance.)

1. Changing eye levels,
   e.g. worm's eye view
2. Stating the problem

3. Themes could be suggested that motivate ideas which emphasise distance

MOTIVATION: Children are asked to focus on an object in the room and imagine themselves a worm on the ground. How would you see this object? Draw a line on your sheet of paper to show the position of the worm and how he would see the object (1). Remember to make the shape stand on the line. This time on the same sheet of paper, pretend that you are a dog, and draw another line to show his position on the paper and how he would see the object. Now draw a line to show your position, and draw the shape the way you see it, on the line. Draw a line to show the level from which a grown-up would see the object.

EVALUATION: Ask the children to examine their drawings and state whether the shapes are near or far away. Now distribute a new sheet of paper. Draw shapes that are near and shapes that are far away (2). Include many things that you think are important to your story (3).

EXPANDING OPPORTUNITIES: To express in a picture the room as seen by a fly on the ceiling.

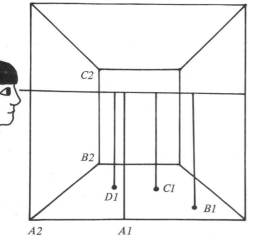 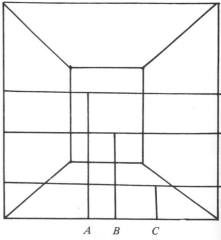

LEARNING SITUATION: Relating different sizes to different areas

PROCESS: Cutting shapes from magazines and pasting them down

MATERIALS: Photographs from magazines, white paper for supports, scissors, paste

LEARNING:

1. Stating the problem
2. Relationship of size to the rectangle
3. Relating the results to real-life situations

MOTIVATION *(Visual and Verbal)*: Ask the pupils to look for and cut out large and small figures from magazines. Distribute two sheets of white paper as supports to each pupil. (Sizes 16.5 x 5cm and 15 x 10cm).

Ask the pupils to place the large cut-out figure on the small sheet, and the small cut-out figure on the large sheet (1). Discuss results (2). What happens to the small figure in the large sheet? How does the large figure 'fit into' the small sheet? What would you have to do with the large figure to make it fit in? Can you alter the figure to make the shape relate to the four sides of the sheet of paper? When you are satisfied with your arrangement paste it down.

Ask the pupils to focus their attentions on the small figure in the larger sheet of paper. How can you change the figure so that it doesn't appear lost in the rectangle?Discuss the possibility of enlarging the figure or adding more figures so that the space is occupied.

EVALUATION: Ask the pupils to discuss similar situations in everyday life, e.g. large furniture in a small room, a grand piano in the kitchen (3).

EXPANDING OPPORTUNITIES: To make an imaginative picture that combines the pupil, his pet animal and a monster.

Page 86: Changing eye levels depending on height of viewer. A = high; B = standing; C = low. A1 = the viewer standing forward, or further back at B1, C1 and D1. From any of these positions the Horizontal Plane A2-B2 and the Vertical Plane B2-C2 will develop.

LEARNING SITUATION: Discovering how to relate unrelated forms

PROCESS: Cutting shapes

MATERIALS: Photographs from old magazines, cartridge paper for support, scissors, paste (cold water)

LEARNING: Relationship

1. A shape   2. Related lines

MOTIVATION: Magazines are distributed and pupils are asked to find action figures (1). What are action figures? Try and find big ones. When you find a number of different actions cut them out and lay them flat on your sheet of white paper. Think how you might change the action. Maybe you could cut a leg off one tiger and place it on another figure. Maybe you could make a standing figure a sitting figure? You might like to change the head. You might replace a small head with a big head.

When you are pleased with the relationships, paste the different parts down. If you have spaces in the background fill them with related lines (2).

EVALUATION: How many were able to relate the figures to the space? Did anyone create a new movement? Does your arrangement of the parts tell a story? Individual pupils are asked to tell their story.

EXPANDING OPPORTUNITIES: Changing the expression by changing the posture.

LEARNING SITUATION: To express an idea through modified colour contrasts of warm to cool

PROCESS: Pasteing fragments of paper in juxtaposition

MATERIALS: An assortment of coloured paper or coloured pages from magazines, paste, spoon, folded magazine paper and cartridge paper 25 x 38cm for support

LEARNING:

1. Stating the problem   2. Procedure

MOTIVATION· Who can name the ways we have painted pictures? Today we are going to plan one by arranging little shapes of colour on a background sheet of paper (1). Can anyone tell me what this kind of picture is called? (Mosaic.) Tear out small shapes of different colours and make bundles of the same colour. When you have all your colours collected you may start 'buttering' them on to make your mosaic. A folded magazine printed page is distributed to each pupil with a spoonful of paste placed on it. The torn shape is dipped in the paste and buttered on to the support (2). Do not forget to use warm and cold colours. Try and make a warm picture or a cold picture. Fill all the paper including the background thinking of your colour arrangement.

EVALUATION: Who made their picture large enough to fill the whole space? Describe what happens when you use warm and cool colours in various areas of your mosaic. Where would you find mosaics today? Were mosaics used in any other buildings besides churches? (Floors in Roman villas.) Show photographs of Byzantine churches.

EXPANDING OPPORTUNITIES: Pupils may recall different experiences from their own life and carry out an idea in mosaic using limited colour schemes.

LEARNING SITUATION: To show balance dependent on dark and light contrast

PROCESS: Cutting (tessera) and designing a mosaic of paper shapes

MATERIALS: Black sugar paper, white grey sugar paper for support, paste, paste containers, scissors, paste brushes

LEARNING:

1. Stating the problem
2. Procedure
3. Vocabulary
4. Contrast
5. Painting

MOTIVATION: Today we will make another mosaic but this time we will use black and white shapes (1). Black and white paper and scissors are distributed. Pupils are asked to cut them into small squares (tessera) (2, 3). You may like to plan a fantastic creature for your mosaic. A sheet of grey sugar paper is distributed for a support. You can make a dark outline by placing the black tessera together or light shapes by placing the white tessera together (4). Try to use the dark and light so that they are related to each other.

EVALUATION: How many have dark parts and light parts in their mosaic? What happened when you placed all light together or all black? Explain how and why you use dark and light? Can we find dark and light in the room? Why must we have dark and light in a picture (5)?

EXPANDING OPPORTUNITIES: 'Changing from day to night', and dark to light tones.

Print from polystirine.

LEARNING SITUATION: To emphasise contrast of line

PROCESS: Painting

MATERIALS: Polystyrine sheets or meat trays, tempera paint, newsprint, carpenter nails and wide, thin rollers, flat surfaces for spreading paint (biscuit tin lids or plastic surfaces)

LEARNING:

1. Teacher demonstration
2. Pupils may be questioned about their subject
3. Dominant and subordinate lines
4. Printing vocabulary

MOTIVATION: Today we will create a picture in lines that we can print (1). How are pictures printed in a book (2)? (Letterpress printing process may be explained.) You may make lines in the back of the polystyrine sheet or meat tray. This will be the printing block. The block may be inked with the roller. Then a sheet of paper is placed flat on the inked surface and pressed with the hand in a rubbing motion. Think of the subject you want to represent and make sure you have important lines (thick) and lines that are not so important (thin) (3).

EVALUATION: Who can tell me what happened to your picture when you took a print? It changed, it reversed from left to right (4). Why are pictures not reversed in the book? Tell me about your picture. I hope you did not forget the important lines?

EXPANDING OPPORTUNITIES: Printing from string pictures.

LEARNING SITUATION: Designing in construction card, shapes to express an idea

PROCESS: Construction

MATERIALS: Construction card of assorted colours, staplers, paper clips, tempera colour, scissors, brushes

LEARNING:

1. Teacher demonstration   2. Relationship of size

MOTIVATION: Today we will imagine a circus. What do you find at the circus? The ring, the animals, clowns, a ring master. We will have groups of four to make the circus. Each group will have to decide what they will have in their circus. We will make the ring first. A strip of construction card is cut 7.5cm wide and bent to form a circle of 30.5cm in diameter and stapled (or clipped) (1). Now we will make the animals and clowns. Sheets of folded construction card are distributed and shapes are cut making sure that top end remains unfolded. Tails and heads of animals may be made separately and attached (1). Shapes are now decorated with lines and when dry are opened and slipped over the ring or leant against the ring.

EVALUATION: Circuses are displayed and groups are asked to explain about them. Does your circus tell us what type it is? Has it got the right scale? Large and small (2). What do we mean by scale? Maybe the clown is too big beside the elephant.

EXPANDING OPPORTUNITIES: Pupils may create paper constructions for a diorama.

Folded construction card.

Animal shapes cut out.

Animals placed in r

LEARNING SITUATION: To unify a design by using harmonising shapes of colour and light

PROCESS: Cutting and painting

MATERIALS: Black sugar paper, tissue paper of assorted colours, adhesive, scissors, paste brushes, felt markers

MOTIVATION: Today you might like to design some see-through (transparent) pictures. We will use these colours (tissue paper). What happens when we hold the tissue up to the light? The light shines through, but we cannot see through clearly (translucent). What happens when we look through two sheets of the same colour? (The colour darkens.) What happens when we look through two different colours? (They change.) We will cut shapes in the black paper. Do not forget to leave black shapes in between your shapes. When you are pleased with your arrangement of shapes select your favourite colours from the tissue paper. Put some paste around the shape on the black paper and stick down the tissue paper. Do not put paste on the tissue paper because the colour bleeds. When you have all the shapes covered, see how you can change some by darkening others. You may like to draw lines in the shapes with markers.

EVALUATION: The translucent pictures are stuck to the windows with adhesive tape. Individual pupils are asked to explain their pictures. What colour did you get when you placed blue over red or yellow over red? Did anybody try green over red? Were some people able to make their colours darker. Would these pictures remind you of something you have seen before? Where did you see it? Where else is coloured light used? (On the stage.) Is there a difference between coloured light and tissue paper? (transparent.)

EXPANDING OPPORTUNITIES: Drawings may be used on white paper, turpentine may then be rubbed on the back of the paper to make a transparency.

LEARNING SITUATION: To organise simple lines and shapes in space, expressing a personal experience

PROCESS: Painting in tempera or crayon drawing

MATERIALS: Tempera colour or crayons, newsprint 30 x 40cm, brushes, crayons, water containers, mixing dishes

LEARNING:

1. Stating the problem   3. Shapes related to space
2. Dominance   4. Identifying background

MOTIVATION: I am sure you would like to tell me about something that happened to you. Maybe a trip you took or a pretend trip. (Travel experience could be discussed) (1). You will make yourself the important part of the story (2). But, there will be many more things that are part of the story. We will look at the air spaces in our picture and we will draw where the story takes place. We will not forget to make some things go out to the edge of the paper (3).

EVALUATION: You all seem to have very interesting stories. Who will tell me about their story? Can we tell the place where the story took place (4)? Why? Does every part of the paper help to tell part of the story?

EXPANDING OPPORTUNITIES: Personal expressions of experiences may be made in many media and various kinds of surfaces or paint with a variety of tools.

LEARNING SITUATION: Discovering that colour, an element of art, has a wide range of hue and tone

PROCESS: Painting

MATERIALS: Tempera paint, newsprint 25 x 38cm, brushes — size 8, jars and mixing dishes, covers for the desks

LEARNING:

1. Mixing primary colours
2. Secondary colours
3. Tertiary colours

4. Light and dark
5. Intermediate colours

MOTIVATION: Do we know what happens when we mix red with blue (violet), blue with yellow (green), yellow with red (orange) (1)? We call this 'mixing the primary colours', — red, yellow, blue, to get secondary colours (2).

Newsprint is distributed and pupils are asked to mix the primary colours. See what happens when you mix the secondary colours — violet and orange (russet), violet and green (olive), orange and green (citron) (3).

Would you like to make a painting using the colours you have discovered? But we will add white to some and black to others. What happens when we add black (4)?

EVALUATION: Individual pupils hold up paintings and are questioned. Did you use olive colour or russet or citron? Where would you find olive colour? (Trees and grass, flowers.) Where would you find russet or citron?

EXPANDING OPPORTUNITIES: Discovering what happens when you mix red with violet — red with orange and blue with green — blue with violet and yellow with green — yellow with orange (5).

LEARNING SITUATION: Understanding the principles of balance, formal or informal (symmetrical or asymmetrical)

PROCESS: Assembling

MATERIALS: Assortment of small boxes, adhesive, card for support, tempera paint, brushes, jar for water, mixing dishes

LEARNING:

1. Teacher demonstration

MOTIVATION: What happens when two objects of equal weight are hung from the opposite ends of a rod (1)? If you have objects of different weight how can you achieve balance? (More suspending string from centre or add shapes to lighter end.) Have we been experimenting with more than one kind of balance?

Select boxes from collection and arrange into formal or informal balance. You may paint them when you are finished.

EVALUATION: Who arranged the boxes in a formal balance? An informal balance? Tell us about your assemblage. Look around the room to see how many examples of formal and informal balance can be found.

Maybe we can find different examples of balance with the side of the window, building, trees, clouds, etc.

EXPANDING OPPORTUNITIES: Creating mobiles with informal balance. Calder's mobiles may be referred to.

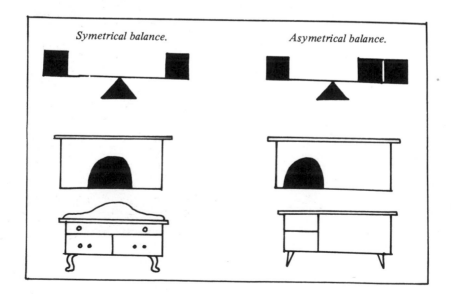

Symetrical balance.

Asymetrical balance.

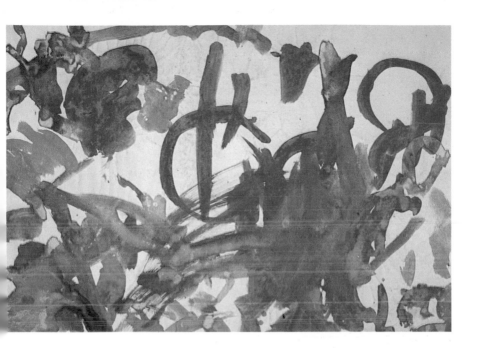

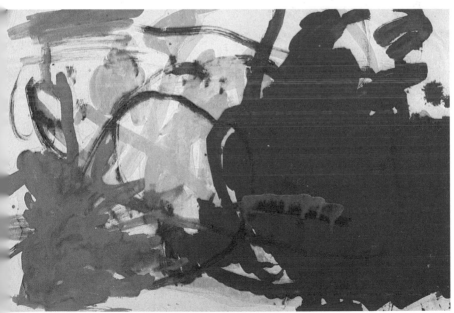

Top: Example of the Motor Act. Drawing does not depend on what it sees. *Bottom:* 'My Dog.' Purely the Motor Act but a good instance of the naming stage. (Junior Infant).

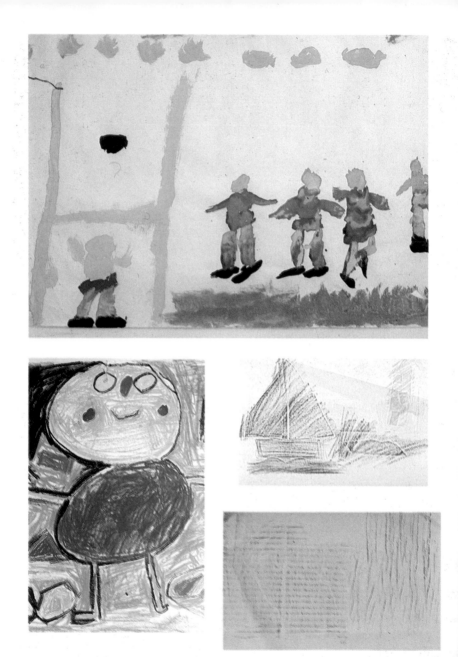

Top: 'Playing football.' Exaggeration of important parts — the boots. (Junior). *Left:* 'Girl.' Emphasis on circles for the figure. (Junior). *Mid-right:* Rubbing shapes. Crayon. See First Class No. 15. (Junior). *Bottom right:* Texture. A surface rubbing. (Junior).

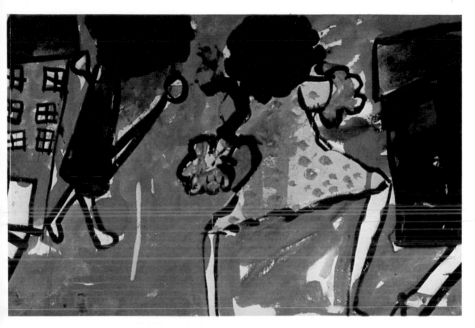

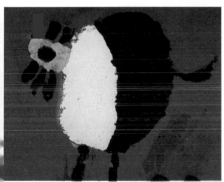

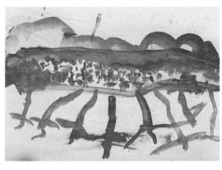

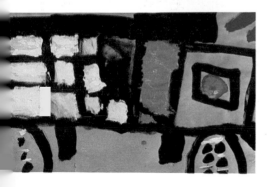

Top: 'Me chasing my sister.' Figure and action powerfully expressed. (Junior). Courtesy Texaco Child Art Competition. *Mid-left:* 'Wonderful Pussy.' Shape emphasis. (Junior). Courtesy Texaco Child Art Competition. *Mid-right:* 'An animal.' (Junior. Age: 5). *Bottom:* 'Big Lorry.' Emphasis on repetition of shape. Interest in pattern. (Junior. Age: 6). Courtesy Texaco Child Art Competition.

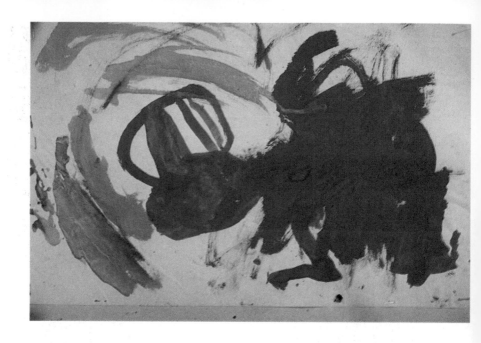

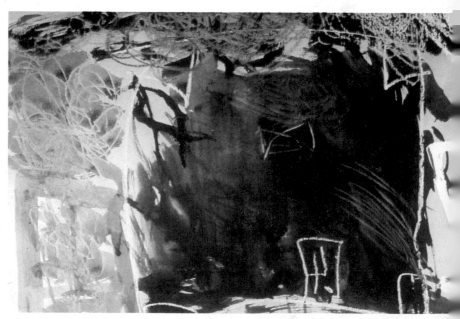

Top: 'A Rabbit.' (Junior. Age: 5). *Bottom:* 'Exploding house.' (Junior. Age: 6)
Courtesy Texaco Child Art Competition.

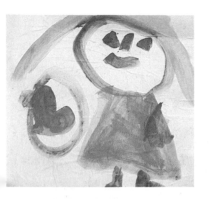 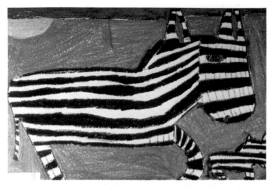

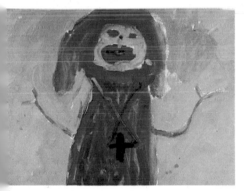 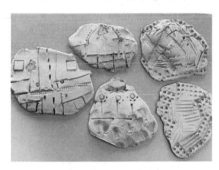

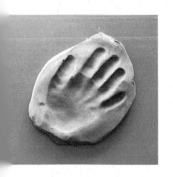 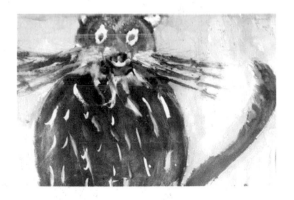

Top left: 'Anna.' Good example of direct brushwork. (Junior. Age: 5). *Top right:* 'Zebra.' Wax crayon. (Junior. Age: 7). Courtesy Texaco Child Art Competition. *Mid-left:* 'My teacher.' Emphasis on important features. (Junior. Age: 7). Courtesy Texaco Child Art Competition. *Mid-right:* Making pictures with clay. (Junior. Age: 9). *Bottom left:* 'My hand.' Imprint on clay. (Junior. Age: 5). *Bottom right:* 'Cat.' A seven year old feeling of a cat. (Junior). Courtesy Texaco Child Art Competition.

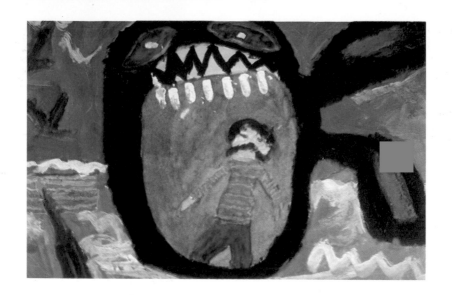

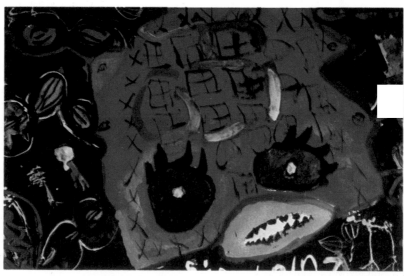

Top: 'Jonah in the whale's belly.' Lively imaginative work. (Junior. Age: 7). Courtesy Texaco Child Art Competition. *Bottom:* 'Crab.' Emotive colour. (Junior. Age: 7). Courtesy Texaco Child Art Competition.

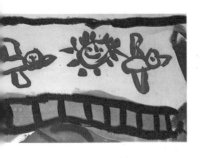

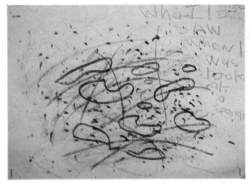

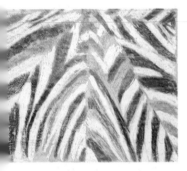

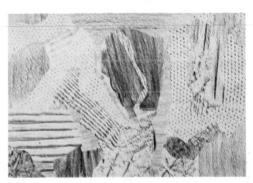

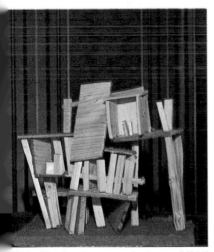

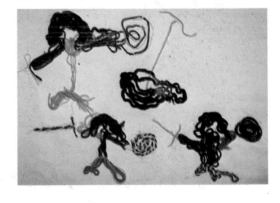

left: The development of schema. (Middle. Age: 8). *Top right:* 'What I saw when ⊃ked at a sponge.' Expressing feeling. See Third Class No. 7. (Middle). *Mid-left:* ⊇loping pattern from leaf. (Middle). *Mid-right:* Picture from surface rubbings. 1dle). *Bottom left:* Space structure from wood oddments. (Middle). *Bottom* : Drawing with yarn. (Middle).

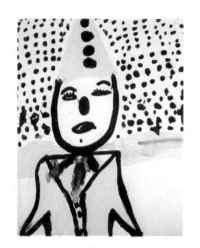
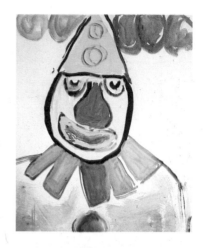
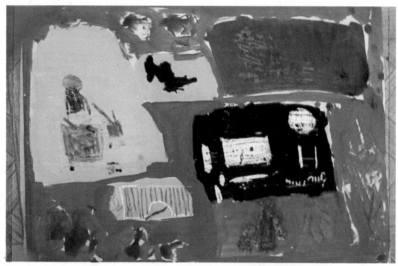
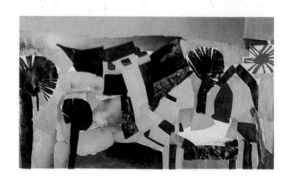

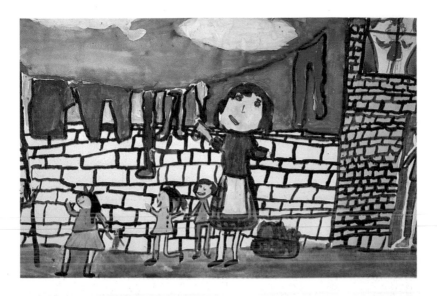

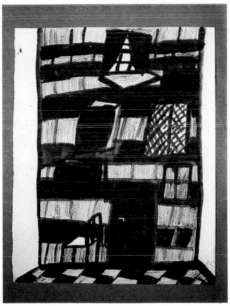

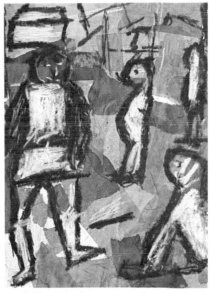

Top: 'Hanging out the washing.' Excellent understanding of scale. (Middle). *Bottom left:* 'Room with chair.' Expressing space. (Middle). *Bottom right:* Mixed media picture. Tissue paper and crayon. (Middle).

Page 104.

Top left: 'Clown.' Combining art elements — line, shape and colour. Line and spot. (Middle). *Top right:* 'Clown.' Combining art elements — line, shape and colour. Line and shape. (Middle). *Centre:* Texture and shape. Crayon and paint. (Middle). *Bottom:* 'Trees and camel.' Cut paper picture (Middle).

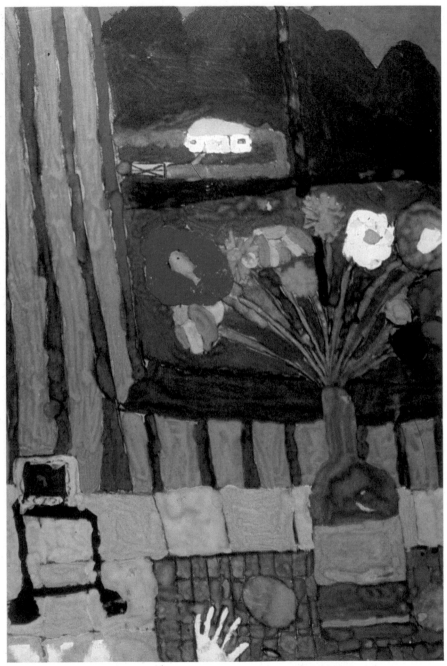

'Flowers at window.' Good colour and pattern. (Middle. Age: 9). Courtesy Texaco Child Art Competition.

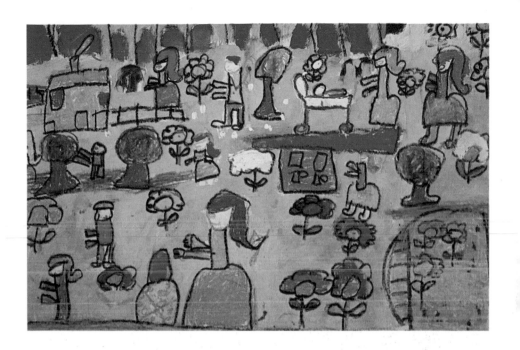

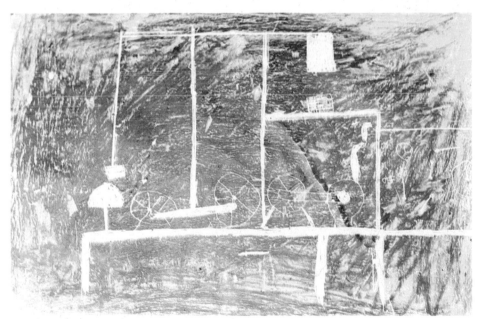

Top: Base line and schema. Note multiple base lines. (Middle). *Bottom:* 'The Machine.' Sgraffito. (Middle. Age: 8).

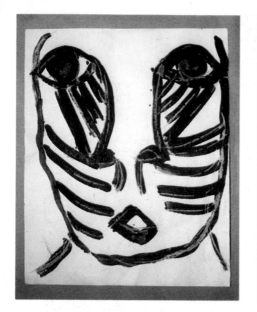
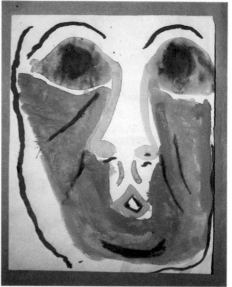
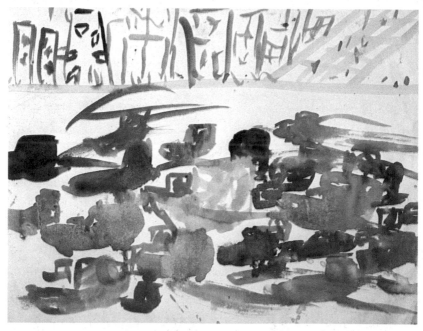

Top left: 'Face.' Expressing shape through the art elements. (Senior). *Top right:* 'Face.' Combining art elements – line, shape and colour. (Senior). *Bottom:* 'Traffic jam.' Pattern and movement. (Senior).

'The Battle.' Note pattern and movement. (Senior).

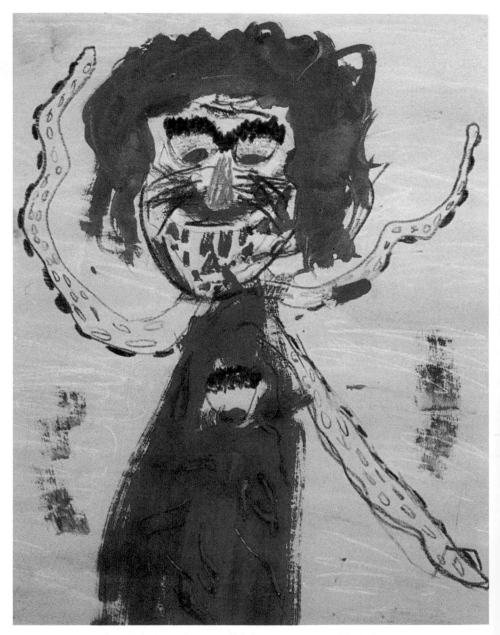

'The Monster.' Expressive line and shape. Cardboard tool and pencil. (Senior).

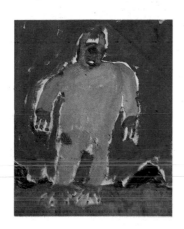

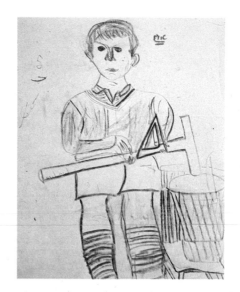

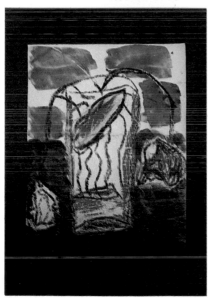

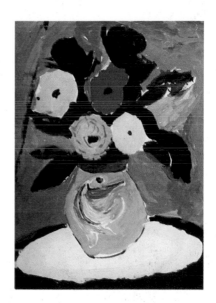

Top left: 'The Monster.' Expressive shape. Painting with brush. (Senior). *Top right:* Figure drawing. Charcoal. (Senior). *Bottom left:* 'Flowers in Vase.' Drawing from observed forms. (Senior). *Bottom right:* 'Flowers in Vase.' Drawing from observed forms. (Senior).

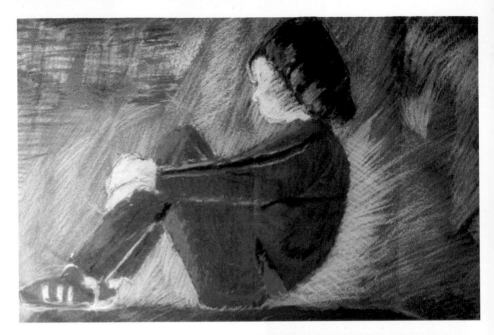

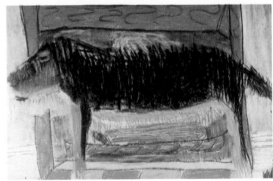

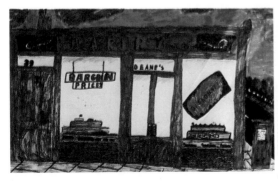

Top: 'Girl in track-suit.' Figure drawing. (Senior. Age: 11). Courtesy Texaco Child Art Competition. *Centre:* 'Dog by fire.' Crayon drawing. (Senior. Age: 11). Courtesy Texaco Child Art Competition. *Bottom:* 'The Bakery.' Good visual recording. (Senior. Age: 11). Courtesy Texaco Child Art Competition.

LEARNING SITUATION: Building a bowl using the pinch clay method, emphasising symmetry

MATERIALS: Pottery clay, corn powder, or plasticine

LEARNING:

1. Symmetry
2. Explaining technique
3. Understanding texture
4. Identifying ceramics

MOTIVATION: How would we make a bowl out of this ball of clay? Teacher demonstrates the pinched method. When bowls are completed (2), the pupils are asked to feel them.

Question: Do you know what we call this feeling? (Texture.) How can we change the texture on the bowl? How can we make it humpy, smooth or rough?

EVALUATION: Who made a rough texture? What did you make it with? Did anybody make a smooth texture? How were they made? Can we find pictures of anything made of clay in our magazines?

EXPANDING OPPORTUNITIES: Texturing slab tiles using raffia, rope, pine cones, small stones etc.

LEARNING SITUATION: To develop pattern by the repetition of shape and colour

PROCESS: Printing with a stamp tool

MATERIALS: Potatoes, tempera colour placed on wet blotting paper, nails or old nail files or blunt nose scissors (for cutting texture surface), paper for covering desks, cleaning-up equipment, rags, newspaper, paper bags

LEARNING:

1. Stating the problem
2. Teacher demonstration
3. Relating to pattern in the environment

MOTIVATION: Let's pretend we are designing wrapping paper for parcels. This wrapping paper will have a printed, all-over pattern and borders (1).

First we will make a printing tool. Potatoes cut in half are distributed to the pupils. They are asked to cut shapes out of the flat surface. (The potato may be textured or incised) (2). Do not forget to collect all the cut away pieces and put them into the bags provided. Press your stamp tool into the ink or paint and then press it onto the paper. Let us try a border first, i.e. we stamp a single row across the paper. Each stamp must join the last one until we fill a row. When one border is finished we might like to try a new one. This time reverse the stamp. New paper is distributed. Fill the sheet and let every row join the last one. Let some of the background paper show through.

EVALUATION: Tell how you arranged your all-over pattern on the background. Did anybody find background shapes? Where do you find patterns with background shapes? Can we find patterns in nature (3)? What makes the pattern on the trees? Can we have a pattern of lines? Is there a pattern of lines in the room? e.g. window, sink, lines on the floor, on clothes, rugs, carpets.

EXPANDING OPPORTUNITIES: Additional printing patterns may be self invented using match boxes, string stuck on match boxes, sticks, etc.

Opposite: Pattern in the environment.

LEARNING SITUATION: Selecting and arranging two-dimensional shapes to create a pattern for a relief print

PROCESS: Relief printing, crayon rubbings

MATERIALS: Construction card, leaves, paper strips, paper clips, newsprint 25 x 38cm, scissors, crayons, cleaning-up equipment, bag for waste paper

LEARNING: Recalling patterns — repetition of day, night, seasons etc.

1. Stating the problem   3. Resultant shapes
2. Process

MOTIVATION: Do we know what a pattern is? Can we find a pattern of line or shape in the room? So pattern is a repetition of a unit. First we will plan a design (1). Any textured surfaces will be good. We will cut shapes in construction card and place them so that we have a repetition on a support or we may arrange leaves, strings, card strips or paper clips (2). When we are satisfied with the pattern, we will place a sheet over the shapes. Keep both papers flat on our desk and hold the two papers together firmly at the bottom with our right hand, move the crayon on its side starting at the bottom of the top paper. When you have rubbed the crayon over the whole top paper you will see a print coming through. Try and rub two or three crayon colours over your top paper. You will see that dark colours make the best prints.

EVALUATION: How did you arrange the shapes on the paper (3)? Did you find 'in between' shapes? Were you able to use one or more colours in your print? Can we find 'in between' shapes in the room? What other word could we use for these shapes?

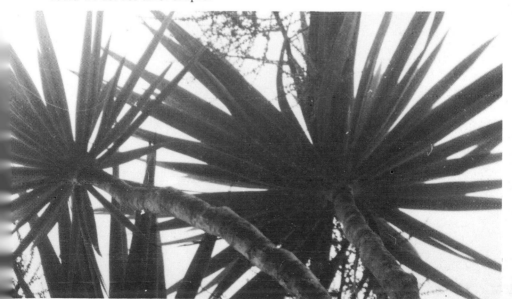

LEARNING SITUATION: To create a three-dimensional form, establishing unity of colour and texture

PROCESS: Building and shaping

MATERIALS: Paper, newsprint, paper such as corrugated and construction card may be used, scissors, stapler, clips, tempera paints, adhesive paste, tape, glue

LEARNING:

1. Statement of the problem   3. Variation
2. Process

MOTIVATION: How would you like to make hats today (1)? Why do people wear hats? Are all hats the same? Are hats of today the same as they used to be long ago? What are the differences? Hats must fit on the head (2). So we will start with the head band. We will cut a strip of paper for the band and measure it around your head. We will cut it then and staple it. What part of the hat comes next? We will make the rim from another strip and attach it to the band. Now the crown — you can decide to make it big, small or any way you like. (Demonstrate how to cut and squeeze paper, simple cuts and overlaps.) What kind of colour will you choose (3)? Maybe some people would like to texture the hat. What type of textures would you find in a hat.

EVALUATION: Does the brim of your hat fit your head? Does the crown stay attached to your head? Discuss how the shapes and colour unify to make a more interesting hat. Can anyone describe a hat that was worn long ago? What date was it? What type of hat did the Romans wear? What type of hats did they wear in the last century? So we know different people wore different hats for social occasions.

EXPANDING OPPORTUNITIES: The unity of colour and shape may be used to create badges or other identifying decorative items.

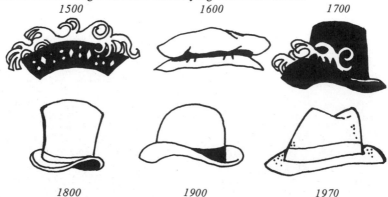

1500   *1600*   *1700*

1800   *1900*   *1970*

LEARNING SITUATION: To describe form in line and contrasting imaginative colour

PROCESS: Drawing and painting

MATERIALS: Chalk, tempera colour, grey sugar paper 25 x 38cm, brushes, mixing dishes, jars for water and cleaning-up materials

LEARNING:

1. Visual recall — imagination   2. Statement of problem

MOTIVATION: Did anybody go very high up and look down on the top of things (1)? What shapes did you see? Today you can imagine yourself high up in the sky, looking down on the tops of things and seeing new shapes. Discuss aerial views, looking down on trees, houses, flower beds, paths, streets, cars, lamp poles and fences. You may make drawings of all the shapes you see from your vantage point arranging them on your paper so that some are standing close together and others standing by themselves with spaces between them (2). You will probably want to cover the chalk lines out with your colours so do not press too hard on the chalk. Use contrasting colours when you paint — make it exciting.

EVALUATION: Who used large shapes and small shapes? Is your painting like a pattern of shapes? Maybe somebody had smaller shapes inside larger shapes. Did you use contrasting colours? What are the contrasts? (Dark and light or contrast of hue.) Where do we find contrasting shapes? Did you enjoy making this kind of painting? Why?

EXPANDING OPPORTUNITIES: Pupils may continue to seek other interesting viewpoints, for example a snail's viewpoint, and this may be interpreted in lines, shapes and colours.

Viewpoint. Form in lines, shapes, colours.

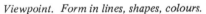

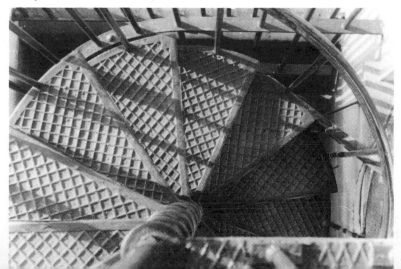

LEARNING SITUATION: To express emotions through line

PROCESS: Drawing with a brush

MATERIALS: Newsprint 25 x 38cm approx., black tempera paint, brushes, jars for water, mixing dishes, newspaper to protect desks and cleaning-up equipment

LEARNING:

1. Recalling an experience   3. Expressive drawing
2. Stating the problem

MOTIVATION: When walking across the road, did anyone ever hear a car horn very close to them? How did you feel? What way was your body when it happened? Pupils are asked to recall similar experiences and situations: happy, sad, excitement, fear (1). Today we will tell with line using the brush and paint about your experiences (2). Remember you are drawing how you felt about your experiences, your own body (3). Try and fill up the sheet of paper with feeling. Your drawing may have exaggeration and distortion. What is exaggeration? When do we exaggerate?

EVALUATION: Pupils are asked to tell about their drawing. What type of lines did you use to describe happy? Are the same lines used to describe fear? What about sad? What do we call this drawing? Reproductions of drawing expressing emotions may be shown.

EXPANDING OPPORTUNITIES: Express a 'visit to the dentist', 'being attacked by a ferocious animal'. Express how you would feel if you were a flower being walked on, or how you felt when you cut your knee. Some of the above could be expressed in comic or cartoon strip.

LEARNING SITUATION: To organise simple symbolic shapes in a composition

PROCESS: Cutting or tearing and arranging shapes

MATERIALS: Coloured construction card, cartridge paper for support, scissors, adhesive paste, cleaning-up materials

LEARNING:

1. Visual recall
2. Relating parts to the whole

3. Observation of essentials
4. Principles of design

MOTIVATION: Did anybody ever go on a tour (1)? We will think about all the exciting things we would see. How would we show a crowd? Would it be a big shape? Would it be several shapes? Would you have different colours to show different people? What about animals? If we saw several animals would they make one shape? Would you see trees and houses? We will cut or tear out shapes to represent one person at a time and then crowd them together on the background paper (2). Would you have all separate parts? No, only the most important parts would be shown. Then we would want to know where you visited. So you will show the place where you visited (trees, houses, sheds, dogs, cows, buses, people) with torn or cut paper shapes (3).

EVALUATION: Were you able to tear or cut strips to look like crowds? Were you able to group the animals to look like one shape? Who got the trees to look like one shape? Do all the shapes seem to be working together to create unity (4)?

EXPANDING OPPORTUNITIES: Further experiences may be described in terms of symbols that are associated with familiar things using the known to explain the new.

Symbolic shapes. Detail from Louis le Brocquy drawing for 'The Tain' (Dolmen Press).

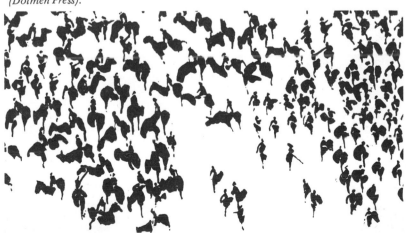

LEARNING SITUATION: To organise figure shapes to express action

PROCESS: Painting

MATERIALS: Tempera colour, cartridge paper, brushes – school fitch size 8, mixing dishes, jars for water, old newspapers for desk protection and cleaning-up materials

LEARNING: Visual movement

1. Recall action
2. Relation of parts to the whole

3. Dominant and subordinate parts of composition

MOTIVATION: Show photographs of people in action. (Large photos from magazines.) Discuss – when a figure is running, what way are the arms, what way are the legs. How about the head? What position is it in? We will think of your favourite sport today. (Pupils are questioned as to their favourite games.) We will paint a picture of your favourite sport showing a lot of actions. Will you have a crowd of people as on-lookers? (Remember the crowd shapes from our last picture.) You can put yourself in the important part of the game. When you begin to paint plan to put yourself in an important spot on the paper. Next important are the other members of the game, you will place them where they can help you with the important action. Try and arrange these figures in interesting spots near the drawing of yourself. Then look at the spaces left on your paper and put lines and shapes in them to show things that are outside, e.g. buildings, trees, fences, grass, seats, flags, poles. When you are painting all these things make them in your own individual way. Do not forget to start with the big shapes and then the small details. So that we have large shapes and small shapes.

EVALUATION: Who was able to fill the paper with big shapes and small helping shapes? Did you make yourself the important shape? What about the spaces in between the shapes? I hope you made full use of them. Who connected all the shapes to each other and to the four edges of the paper? What colours did you use in the massing of the shapes? Why did you use that particular colour?

EXPANDING OPPORTUNITIES: Pupils may select aspects of everyday experiences and express them, e.g. buying clothes, working in the garden, doing something in the home – washing clothes, etc.

LEARNING SITUATION: Developing an understanding of linear treatment of a subject

PROCESS: Drawing

MATERIALS: Newsprint 25 x 38cm, tempera colour, any flexible material, cardboard strip, felt markers, sponge strips or charcoal, dishes, jars for water and cleaning-up material

LEARNING:

1. Kinetic recall   3. Process
2. Stating the problem

MOTIVATION: If you suddenly fell down the stairs or if you went swirling up in the air, what kind of line would you use to describe it (1)? (Discuss various imaginary situations and let each pupil choose a situation.) Show on your paper the kind of lines that would tell how you felt (2). Would it be thin, delicate, strong? Would it be twisting, swaying from one side to another? Would it be spiraling? What is spiraling? What direction would it take? (Vertical, horizontal.) Maybe you would like to cut your paper into a thin panel or a wide panel. Think what best would suit your 'feelings'. If you have background spaces in between the lines you may fill them in with related lines, that is lines that move in a similar way to the main lines. Would we make these lines as strong as the main lines? No. If you are using charcoal we must fix it in case it may rub (3). You may put a very light colour wash over the whole paper.

EVALUATION: Who made their 'feeling' line strong? Is there a movement covering the entire surface? What about the in-between areas, did we make the lines interesting in size and colour? What colour 'wash' did you brush on the whole design and why? Were lines ever used like this long ago to express movement? Examples may be shown of Newgrange, high cross decoration, Maori decoration etc.

EXPANDING OPPORTUNITIES: Similar lines and shapes and colours may be used to convey various moods.

LEARNING SITUATION: Grouping various geometric shapes to create a subject matter

PROCESS: Arranging, relating, painting

MATERIALS: An assortment of small boxes, e.g. match boxes, cigarette boxes, etc., cartridge paper 25 x 38cm, tempera colour paints or crayons, cleaning-up materials

LEARNING: Verbal motivation — Visual motivation

1. Statement of problem
2. Visual recall

3. Relating to everday experience

MOTIVATION: Things that are grouped tend to be seen together. What does that mean? It means clustering, distance, intervals, space. The small boxes are distributed and a sheet of cartridge paper for a support to each pupil. They are now asked to group them on the paper so that the large ones are all together and the small together. When pupils understand the concept of clustering, intervals, and distance, the boxes are collected and pupils are asked to draw rectangles clustering, with intervals and distance on the sheet of paper (1). As you look at your shapes think of something we see every day, then add any lines or other shapes. Don't forget to make some colours dark and some light. Repeat the colours in three or more parts of your picture.

EVALUATION: Would anybody like to tell me how they started with the space filling rectangular shapes? Why did you start there? Did you find that there were spaces left over? What did you do with them? How many times did you repeat colours? Would we find similar arrangements every day and where (2)? What shape is this school? How is it arranged in the space? How are the windows arranged in the sides of the building (3)?

EXPANDING OPPORTUNITIES: Pupils may be asked to create simple three-dimensional constructions using geometric shapes, with emphasis on the relationship of size and space.

LEARNING SITUATION: Discovering space and expressing a form in space (Expressing space on a flat surface)

PROCESS: Building, glueing, slotting, scoring, drawing and painting

MATERIALS: Large cardboard boxes, sheets of light strawboard, adhesive, tempera paint, scissors, crayons, brushes

LEARNING:

1. Stating the problem
2. Introducing the activity
3. Subordinate
4. Positive and negative
5. Additive and subtractive

MOTIVATION: The pupils are asked to arrange the furniture to create space in different ways, e.g. to include small spaces that could be crawled through (1).

This could also include space within spaces. Some of the spaces may be hidden so that they cannot move through them. Perhaps these spaces open out into other spaces or they are surrounded by other spaces (2). Can you make entrances and exits? Individual groups could be asked to move through these spaces while other groups are observing the movement. This could be done on a rotation basis allowing all the pupils to participate in the special experience.

Using the cardboard boxes or sheets of cardboard, try and make a construction that would show all the different spaces that you moved through.

Slotting, cutting, scoring and folding techniques could be introduced at this stage. The finished construction may be painted.

EVALUATION: How many found that their construction spread out horizontally or went up? Is there any difference between them? Did anyone express different levels? Are there any spaces hidden from view (3)? Are there inside and outside spaces (4)? How do they relate? How many people found that they had to add pieces, or subtract pieces (5)? What effect did the paint have on the construction? Were there sections lost when it was painted? Would these constructions suggest ideas for some practical use? Make drawings showing how these constructions could be used?

EXPANDING OPPORTUNITIES: Expressing near and far, upward and downward movement in space, some known space.

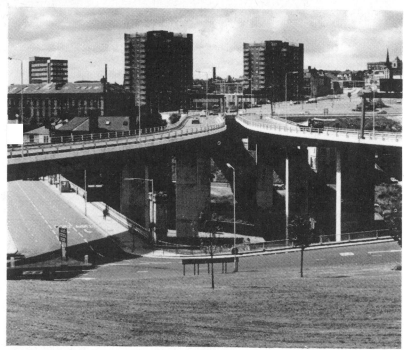

Open and closed spaces in urban environment.

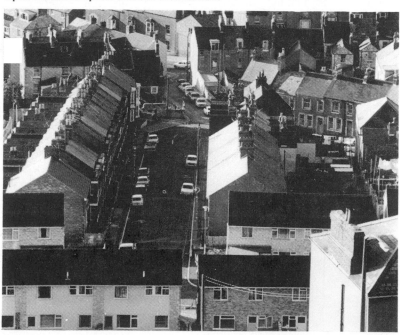

THIRD CLASS

Art Growth Characteristics

1. Growing out of egocentric stage.
2. Likes to work independently and has a greater attention span.
3. Can represent objects more realistically.
4. Beginning to understand how objects really look in their environment.
5. Is aware of the three-dimensional space but does not express it in perspective.
6. Likes design and arrangement.
7. Can describe similarities and differences.
8. Likes to experiment with various tools.
9. Has natural curiosity to explore.
10. Uses colour more realistically.
11. Has an increasing involvement with the function and appearance of his own body.
12. Greater interest in group activity.

Behavioural Objectives (Intended outcome for the pupil)

The pupil will be able to:
Understand open and closed space
Express in dominant and subordinate line
Understand foreground and background
Understand how to express sensory perception
Understand the relationship of form and space
Understand how to create forms in space
Understand the effect of time and how it brings about change
Understand that projections cast shadows
Understand symbols

The pupil will gain control and manipulate media and tools:
Drawing with a variety of tools
Cut and arrange shapes
Construction with discarded materials
Resist crayon painting
Tissue paper painting
Photo-montage
Constructing a string printing block
Stencilling
Crayon etching (Sgraffito)

Learning Situations

1. Discovering how lines can create open and closed spaces.
2. Discovering dominant and subordinate lines.
3. To discover open and closed areas in a relief panel.
4. To show the relationship between background and foregound shapes.
5. To design a surface decoration for a three-dimensional form.
6. Discovering the linear qualities within a leaf and expressing the leaf in a personal way through line.
7. Discovering that taste can be expressed through line.
8. Discovering space and expressing forms in space.
9. Exploring the sense of sound — expressing sound through shape and developing the creative imagination.
10. Exploring the sense of smell — expressing smell through colour and shape.
11. Discovering that action can be employed if images are presented in a particular way.
12. To express the effect of time and the way it changes the shapes of materials and things.
13. To express a form that moves slowly in space.
14. Discovering balance and shape relationship as well as movement.
15. Creating a rhythmic arrangement through contrast of warm and cold coloured shapes.
16. Expressing colour as a felt experience.
17. Relating colour to mood — depicting the different characteristics of personalities.
18. Introducing the process of stencilling. Showing the relationship between figure and ground.
19. Expressing an idea through a continuous linear organisation.
20. Creating images based on sound.
21. To create a picture expressing time and change (Story in frame form).
22. To discover the effect of light on a three-dimensional form.
23. Expressing emotions through facial expressions.
24. Discovering the necessity of symbols or a quick way of reading.

LEARNING SITUATION: Discovering how lines can create open and closed spaces

PROCESS: Painting

MATERIALS: Tempera paint (dark colour), brushes, paper support 25 x 38cm

LEARNING: Perceiving

1. Positive and negative
2. Shape enclosed by contour, positive
3. Shape enclosed by contour, negative
4. Stating the problem
5. Interchangeable

MOTIVATION: *(Verbal and Visual)*: While we are describing objects in the room, we draw lines around them. Can you look at the objects in the room and see if there are spaces between them? Can we describe the spaces between the objects with a line also (1)? We will call the space inside the line describing the object the closed space (2) and the space between the objects the open space (3).

Can you show in your sheet of paper the enclosed spaces and the open spaces (4)? Paint the enclosed spaces dark and the open spaces light.

EVALUATION: Are the darker shapes more dominant than the lighter shapes, or is it the other way around (5)? Where else can we find open and closed spaces, e.g. looking from the inside to outside, parks in built-up areas, dark spaces and light spaces in a photograph. Empty spaces and full spaces.

EXPANDING OPPORTUNITIES: Make a cardboard model of the school showing open and closed spaces.

LEARNING SITUATION: Discovering dominant and subordinate lines

PROCESS: Cutting, arranging, pasting

MATERIALS: White support 25 x 38cm, black sugar paper or poster paper or any other, dark coloured paper, scissors, paste brushes and paste (poly-cell wallpaper adhesive distributed in small containers)

LEARNING: Perceiving

1. Size relationships
2. Short

3. Dominant and subordinate lines

MOTIVATION: *(Verbal and Visual)*: Make an arrangement of boxes of different sizes on a desk top. Let us look at all the vertical lines in this arrangement of boxes. Which vertical lines are more important (1)? Are some longer or shorter than others? What lines are not so important (2)?

Distribute a sheet of dark coloured paper and a sheet of lighter coloured paper for a support. Can you cut wide strips for the important lines? Can you arrange these strips on the light coloured paper so that you have important lines and less important lines (3)? When you have them arranged to your satisfaction, paste them down.

EVALUATION: (Identify important lines as dominant lines and not so important lines as subordinate lines.) Can we now look for dominant lines in our surroundings? What are the dominant lines in the building, in the street?

EXPANDING OPPORTUNITIES: Make a picture of your street, town, or city showing dominant buildings and subordinate buildings.

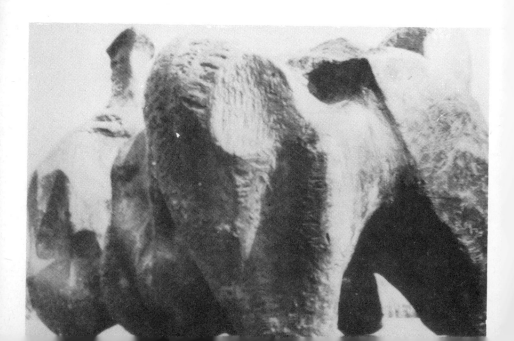

LEARNING SITUATION: To discover open and closed area in a relief panel .

PROCESS: Relief panel building with cardboard shapes which are cut and glued together. Finished panel may be painted or used as a block for printing

MATERIALS: Cardboard support 30 x 25cm, one extra piece of cardboard for relief shapes, PVA glue diluted to a creamy consistency with water and distributed in jars, glue, brushes, scissors, paint brushes

LEARNING: Perceiving
(Previous activity – creating background and foreground shapes; present activity – building open and closed area in relief.)

1. Henry Moore   2. Stating the problem

MOTIVATION: Children are given two sheets of cardboard each, one to be used as a support and the other piece to be cut up into shapes with straight and curved edges for relief building.

When you have the shapes cut, arrange them on your cardboard support so that they touch one edge and one another, and some may touch two other shapes (in-between shapes). The part of the background that is left untouched we will call 'open', and the shapes that are the top surface we will call 'closed'.

Children are asked to paste down shapes when they are satisfied that they have interesting 'open' and 'closed' spaces. The open and closed spaces may be painted as a further enrichment and decoration of the surface (2).

EVALUATION: Ask the children to recall where they have seen open and closed spaces, e.g. spaces between railings, open and closed spaces in buildings, wall plaques, sculpture (1).

EXPANDING OPPORTUNITIES: To create a cardboard structure by cutting and slotting in such a way that when arranged will open spaces into other spaces and enclose spaces.

Reclining figure by Henry Moore. Form and space fluctuate through the inclusion of open space in the form.

LEARNING SITUATION: To show the relationship between background and foreground shapes

PROCESS: Cutting and tearing paper and pasting it down

MATERIALS: Suitable light and dark coloured paper, paste, paste brushes

LEARNING: Perceiving

1. Why object appears lost
2. The background is the same
   – the background is different
3. Figure and background
4. Further examples may be given to amplify above, for example cloud formation, light in reflection, a light in a dark area
5. Stating the problem

MOTIVATION: *(Visual and Verbal)*: Demonstration: two sheets of the same cartridge paper, one large and one small. Paste the small sheet down on the larger sheet with cellulose paste. Ask the children what happens to the smaller piece of paper (1). Does it appear to be lost? What would you have to do with the small piece to make it stand out? Can we see examples of this happening everyday? The bird is lost in the leaves of the branch. Why can't we see the caterpillar? How do we see the butterfly (2)?

Direct the children to the silhouetted objects on the window sill. Establish that the object is dark against a lighter background. We call the shape that is in front the figure, and what is behind it the background (3, 4).

Distribute two sheets, one dark and one light, and ask the children to arrange dark shapes on the light ground and light shapes on the dark ground (5).

Some of the shapes must touch the edge of the background or touch each other.

EVALUATION: Ask the children questions to establish their understanding of background and foreground shapes in the environment.

EXPANDING OPPORTUNITIES: Creating a pattern of dark and light with equal and unequal amounts.

LEARNING SITUATION: To design a surface decoration for a three-dimensional form

PROCESS: Construction

MATERIALS: Small boxes and bags, toilet roll centres, string, adhesive tape, construction card, tempera paint, scissors, brushes

MOTIVATION: You enjoyed painting the fantastic bird. Now I am sure you would like to construct a three-dimensional bird. We will think of them as magic birds. We will make the body of the birds with boxes. We will insert a cardboard tube into the box so that we can carry it. For the wings we will use construction card and stuff small bags for the head. When you have the construction finished we will decorate it with paint.

EVALUATION: We will have a parade with our magic birds. What do our birds stand for? Do they mean anything? What countries use birds to represent them? (German Eagle, American Eagle.) When did people carry birds in a parade? (Roman standards, Egyptian funeral procession, New Guinea festivals.) Photographs would help here.

EXPANDING OPPORTUNITIES: Creating birds in clay.

LEARNING SITUATION: Discovering the linear qualities within a leaf and expressing the leaf in a personal way through line

PROCESS: Drawing with a variety of tools

MATERIALS: Paper, newsprint 30 x 40cm or any other smooth finish paper, tempera paint, yarns, string, crayon, tubes of glue, brushes, strips of cardboard, sponges of varying thickness, assorted sticks. (The class could be broken up into smaller units according to the materials and tools available.)

LEARNING: Perceiving

1. Observing
2. Comparing
3. Contrasting
4. Selecting

5. Terminology
6. Relating
7. Lines to the size of space (format)

MOTIVATION: What sort of leaf have you got? Where did it come from? What shape is it (1)? How big is it? How wide? How small (2)? How many lines can you count on your leaf? Are they all the same length (3)? Are they all straight? How would you like to make a new leaf with the different lines you found in your leaf? Pick some lines you would use (4).

We must draw these lines on the paper. How will you place them on the paper? Will the longest lines go to the edge of the paper? Maybe you would like to make some of the lines move across the paper and maybe some lines will touch one another. Pupils may identify these lines as vertical, horizontal, diagonal, straight, curved (5). Compare these lines with the lines in your clothes or the lines in the class room (6).

EVALUATION: Was there any difference between the line made by the brush and the line made with the strip of cardboard? What was the difference between the lines made with the cord and the yarn? Did anyone use thick and thin lines? How many of you were able to make the leaf fill the paper (7)? Do the lines tell us something about the leaf?

EXPANDING OPPORTUNITIES: Discovering contour lines in nature. Pupils attention is directed to the leaf structure and the lines that describe the contour. Do the lines on the inside tell you anything about the outside line? (Contour.) When the inside lines change do they make the outside lines change? (Do the inside structure lines influence the contour?) Where else would you find this? (Supports in buildings, scaffolding, framework for windows in churches and houses etc.) Where does the inside line start in the leaf and where does it end? Does it move outwards or inwards? Invent a new leaf which tells you what the line on the outside does. Can you make the leaf tell something wonderful, sad, funny, or ordinary?

Page 133 Top: The effects of the ribs and leaf shape.
A: Contour is pushed out by rib lines.
B,C,D: The inner form changes the outer form.

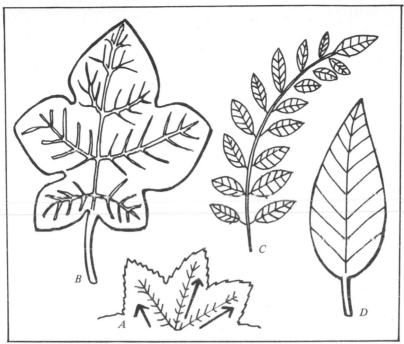

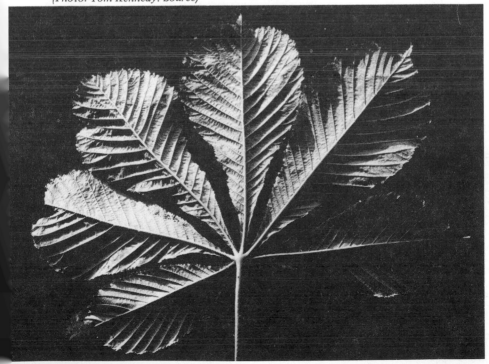

LEARNING SITUATION: Discovering that taste can be expressed through line

PROCESS: Drawing

MATERIALS: Crayons, tempera paint, newsprint 25 x 38cm, brushes, strips of cardboard, sponges

LEARNING:

1. Direct sensory experience
2. Contrast
3. Lines that express movement
4. Terminology
5. Introducing the activity

MOTIVATION: A variety of seed may be distributed to the pupils to taste, for example caraway, fennel, sunflower. Children are questioned as follows: How does it taste (1)? What was it like? How did you feel when you tasted it? In what way do the seeds differ in taste (2)? Can we think of the taste as a line travelling about? What sort of lines do you think will show it (3)? Name the types of line (curved, ziz-zag, straight, flowing, smooth, sharp, thick, thin) (4). How will the lines move on the sheet of paper? (In and out, up and down.) Think of the lines you will use to show the movement of the taste. Arrange these lines so as to give a picture of the taste. Make sure some of the lines go out to the edge of the paper (5).

EVALUATION: How many used thick and thin lines? Did you make the lines go out to the edge of the paper? When you look at the lines on your paper can you tell the taste from them? Why did you use that type of line? Who was able to show a movement from side to side or up and down? Did anybody find that they made shapes? What makes a shape? (A contour line.)

EXPANDING OPPORTUNITIES: Using lines to express feeling and emotions (expressing the emotive line within the object).

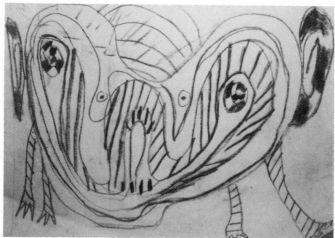

'Fierce Dog.'
Line in
charcoal.

LEARNING SITUATION: Discovering space and expressing forms in space

PROCESS: Recreating in miniature a three-dimensional subject

MATERIALS: Shoe boxes or boxes of a similar size, match boxes, twigs, corks, small stones, sponges, paper, adhesive, scissors

LEARNING:

1. Stating the problem
2. Teacher shows shoe box to the class
3. Spatial relationships
4. Scale of shape and colour
5. Grouping
6. Scale of shape and colour in painting

MOTIVATION: Today we are going to make a diorama (1). Who knows what a diorama is? A diorama is usually set in a box that has one side open (2). When you turn it on one side, that side becomes a base for support, it also has a background which you may like to paint. In this space we are going to create a scene. It may be from your neighbourhood or it may show something from the past. We will all have to think carefully. We will also have to think of the sizes of the objects we are placing in the space. If we are making a tree we must relate it to the space (3). Maybe you could make figures for your scenes, if you do, you will have to think of their height in relationship to the space (4). When pupils have selected their scenes, materials are distributed and pupils are asked to create forms for their dioramas.

EVALUATION: Was everybody able to 'fit' the objects in the space? By that is meant 'are the objects the right scale'. Why do architects draw houses to scale? Who thought about the grouping of the objects (5)? Is grouping important? Why? Where else do we see objects grouped? (Packaging in a supermarket, furniture in a room.) Some reproductions may be examined to see how the art elements are grouped and their scale. Photographs may be examined for scale and grouping. Is scale important in paintings (6)?

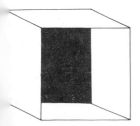

Box with open front.

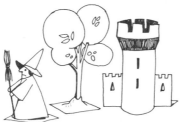

Shapes cut out with base attached.

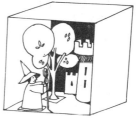

Shapes related and arranged in space.

135

LEARNING SITUATION: Exploring the sense of sound, expressing it through shape and developing the creative imagination

PROCESS: Cutting, tearing, arranging, pasting

MATERIALS: Assortment of coloured surfaces, paper for support, scissors and paste

LEARNING:

1. Recalling
2. Terminology – Contrasting
3. Stating the problem
4. Relating
5. Terminology – Background

MOTIVATION: Did you ever hear a car horn near you when you were crossing the road (1)? What did you do? How did you feel? How did your whole body react? When you listen to music how does your body react? (If possible play different types of music and judge reactions.) Do you react the same to all sounds? When we hear the voice of someone we know, we can recognise who it is. We get a picture of them. We do this with every sound, though we do not see it.

Sound can have shapes – e.g. invisible shapes. Listen to this sound. (Place some objects in a tin can and shake.) Is it heavy, light, sharp, dull, long or short? What shape could this have? Discuss shapes, sharp shapes, round shapes, big, small, smooth, curved or jagged. Do you find in the sound, large shapes or small shapes (2)? How many small shapes can you count? Can you cut and tear the various papers to make these shapes (3)? Remember to use different types.

Can you arrange the shapes on the paper now? Why will they not all fit? (Some are too big and others are too small.) What must we do to make them fit? (Relate the size of the shapes to the format.) We will arrange them so as to give a picture of the sound. Maybe we will find new shapes between our shapes (4).

EVALUATION: Why had we to change the shapes? Where else do we fit shapes? (Furniture in the room, buildings on the site, books in the case. We ourselves are shapes, we must fit in the chair.) How many found background shapes (5)? Have we got contrasting shapes?

EXPANDING OPPORTUNITIES: Creating new shapes from two or more shapes (hybrid shapes). Different shapes, different sounds, shapes that repeat.

LEARNING SITUATION: Exploring the sense of smell, expressing smell through colour and shape

PROCESS: Painting

MATERIALS: Tempera paint, assorted colours, brushes, jars for water, mixing dishes, paper support 25 x 38cm

LEARNING: Perceiving and expressing

1. Relating
2. Identifying
3. Stating the problem
4. Terminology — background, contrasting
5. Individuality

MOTIVATION: Various scents are placed in bottles. Solid pieces can be broken and put into the bottles, e.g. pine, mint, hay, sawdust, flowers, spices, perfumes and providers.

Today we are going to explore the sense of smell. Did anybody ever smell smoke? What was it like (1)? Was it pleasant? What would you say a pleasant smell was? Can you have sour smell, or sharp smells? Could you describe a smell as mellow? What other types of smell can you have?

The bottles are now distributed and the pupils are asked to identify the smell and relate it to a colour and shape. What is a sharp shape and what colour would it have (2)?

The paper, paints, brushes etc. are now distributed and the pupils are asked to show contrasting 'smells' on the paper (3). (Colour — shapes.) Do not forget how you are placing these shapes on the paper, make some go out to the edge. Maybe you will paint the background in contrasting hue (dark and light) to your smell shape (4).

EVALUATION: Individual students are questioned about their painting. The pupils are asked to identify the different smells. Why did you use that colour for that smell? Would everybody use that colour for that particular smell (5)? Why? Did we think of contrasting smells and did we show the contrast on the paper? Is the contrast in the shape or colour?

EXPANDING OPPORTUNITIES: Pupils may express smells they can recall through developing lines, shapes and colours in designs that convey various smells (a smell picture).

LEARNING SITUATION: Discovering that action can be employed if images are presented in a particular way

PROCESS: Crayon etchings

MATERIALS: Assorted coloured crayons, cartridge paper, cocktail sticks or nails

LEARNING:

1. Recalling
2. Teacher demonstration
3. Terminology — crayon.etching
4. Stating the problem
5. Visual clues

MOTIVATION: Who can tell me what happens to the smoke when the wind blows (1)? The smoke moves with the wind and it can tell us which way the wind is blowing. How does a tree move in the wind? When we see a tree bent over we know that the day is windy and the tree is moving. Does the wind blow at the same strength all the time? (Different strengths of wind produce different effects, e.g. a lake, the sea waves, the rain, etc. When a wheel moves at different speeds it changes.

Today we will make a picture that tells about movement or the effect of movement. Demonstration of crayon etching — the paper is covered completely with light tone crayon and then covered with a black crayon — better results are got if the crayon is held on its side (2). Lines are scratched into the dark surface with cocktail sticks or nails. We call this crayon etching (3). Crayons and cartridge paper is now distributed and pupils are asked to fill the sheet with lines showing the effect of movement (4).

EVALUATION: Individual students are asked to hold up their crayon etchings and the class is asked to identify the movements. Are there any differences in the movements? Can we see different strengths of wind? How many made the movement fill the paper? What did we discover? We can tell a lot about things if we draw them in a particular way (5).

EXPANDING OPPORTUNITIES: Observing the changes on coins or pieces of bent wire by spinning them and then drawing them.

LEARNING SITUATION: To express the effect of time and the way it changes the shapes of materials and things

PROCESS: Resist crayon painting

MATERIALS: Assorted coloured crayons, tempera colours, brushes, water, cartridge paper

LEARNING:

1. Perceiving
2. Teacher demonstration
3. Stating the problem
4. Relating shapes to sheet of paper
5. Vocabulary

MOTIVATION: Who can tell what causes a piece of wood to rot? (Time.) What effect has this on the wood? (The shape, colour, size and texture changes.) How does a seed change when you plant it? Who can name other things whose appearance is affected by time? With caution a match could be lit and the change could be demonstrated by allowing it to burn (1).

Crayon resist painting is now demonstrated by applying the crayon to the paper and painting a diluted wash of tempera colour over the paper (2).

Materials are now distributed and pupils are asked to think of something and how it changes with time, and show it on the paper (3).

EVALUATION: Is your paper filled up with your picture (4)? Individual pupils are asked to show the class. Can we tell from the painting what is happening? What word would we use to describe the change? (Erosion, weathering, withering, rotting, rusting) (5).

EXPANDING OPPORTUNITIES: Expressing change by destruction — crushing, pressing.

LEARNING SITUATION: To express a form that moves slowly in space

PROCESS: Painting (direct with a brush in colour)

MATERIALS: Tempera paint, large bristle brushes, dishes for paint and water, cleaning-up material

LEARNING:

1. Recall
2. Imagination
3. Size relationship
4. Background
5. Relating to the environment

MOTIVATION *(Verbal)*: Who can name something that moves very slowly? (A machine or an insect.) How are the parts of it put together (1)? Does it have handles? Maybe it has legs. How do the legs move? Have they got different parts? Can you see it in your mind's eye? Maybe some people would like to use their imagination and invent something that moves slowly (2). How big is this thing (3)? Think what colour it is, is it the same colour all over? Has it eyes or has it lamps?

Paper and paints are now distributed to each pupil. Pupils are asked to draw direct with the brush and show where the thing is (4).

EVALUATION: Individual students are asked to tell about their invention. How did you develop the line in your painting? What shapes did you use? Why did you use that colour? Did you paint in the background? Who made it stand out from the background? Can things that move slowly be always seen? Tell me something that can hide in the background and moves slowly (5). Did you use all the space up in your paper?

EXPANDING OPPORTUNITIES: 'Things change as you walk past them'. Paper is folded into corrugation and straight lines are painted on the right hand side and curves on the left hand side.

LEARNING SITUATION: Discovering balance and shape relationship as well as movement

PROCESS: Designing a mobile with contrasting shapes

MATERIALS: Straw board, long cocktail sticks, strong thread, blunt needles for making holes

LEARNING:

1. Stating the problem

MOTIVATION: Today we are going to make a mobile. Who knows what a mobile is? (It is a type of sculpture that is hung from the ceiling, it moves and it has shapes that relate to one another.) Let us look around the room and find shapes that are related. The shapes are part of a whole shape, e.g. the leaves in the tree are small shapes in the big shape of the tree. Who can find a big shape in the room that has small shapes in it? When you have found the shapes you like best that are related, draw them on the cardboard. Then cut them out. You will require seven or nine shapes.

This is how we will put our mobile together. First take one cocktail stick and tie a string at each end of it. Place it on the desk and cut the strings so that they are even. Now tie a string in the centre of the stick but make it much shorter than the other two. Tie one small shape to the end of it. (The hole is made with the needle.) Next take two more cocktail sticks and tie two more strings on each end of them, keeping them an even length. Then string a shape to each thread. Now we have five shapes tied on. We must balance them now by placing them flat on the desk and tie the first two strings to the second two cocktail sticks. If we do not find the right place to tie them, they will not be balanced. So think about it. You may proceed from this and add as many sticks and shapes as you like. When the mobiles are completed, they may be painted and suspended from a string that is stretched across the room.

EVALUATION: Are the mobiles all moving? If not, why not? Look and see if the shapes overlap as they move? What is overlapping? (Overlapping is when one hides the other.) Where do we find things that overlap? Does anybody know who made the first mobile? His name was Alexander Calder and he made it in 1926 out of metal. It depended on the air to move it. Does yours move by the flow of air? How could we make them move faster? (By heating the air.) They are used today for advertising.

EXPANDING OPPORTUNITIES: Paint shapes that are overlapping and make a relief panel with straw board.

LEARNING SITUATION: Creating a rhythmic arrangement through a contrast of warm and cold coloured shapes

PROCESS: Painting with coloured paper

MATERIALS: Narrow strips of coloured paper torn from magazines in warm and cool colours, paste or glue, surface material — cartridge paper or construction card, scissors, paste sticks (cardboard pieces for application)

MOTIVATION: We all know there are many different ways to make pictures. Today we are going to make one by arranging cut or torn pieces of paper. We will paste them down on a background paper. We will try and arrange them so as to produce a rhythm. Who can tell how you could make a rhythm? (Clapping hands in a regular beat.) How could we show that on the paper? Warm — cold — warm — cold — that is too regular. We will make it more exciting by giving it variations such as we find in music. Tear off small shapes of coloured paper and paste them down to create your own rhythm. Fill the whole sheet leaving no background.

EVALUATION: Did you make your picture large enough to fill the whole space? Describe the rhythm you made with the coloured shapes? Would this type of picture remind you of something you have seen before? What would you call it? Yes, it is called a paper mosaic.

EXPANDING OPPORTUNITIES: Using limited colour schemes, pupils may express their own experiences and carry out their ideas in paper mosaics.

Rhythm in objects.

Also note texture,

line, space-shape, light.

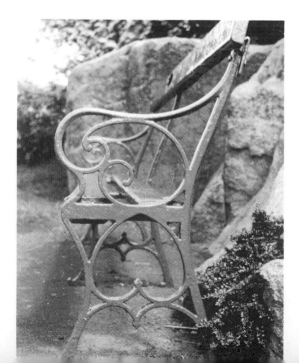

LEARNING SITUATION: Exploring colour as a felt experience

MATERIALS: Flowers, crayons, paints, paper, fabrics, dyes, etc.

LEARNING:

1. Stating the problem
2. Colour weight (dark — light) tone
3. Progression and regression of colour with warm and cold colours
4. Terminology (transparent — opaque)
5. Emotive content of colour
6. Harmonise
7. Tonal range of hues

MOTIVATION: Pupils are asked to examine flowers. (Flowers, because of their direct appeal to our sense of smell, colour and touch, waken our feelings and emotions.) The pupils are then asked to focus their attention on the colours, smells and textile qualities within the flowers.

Do the colours in the petals change or blend? Which colours appear heavy and which appear light? Where do we find the heavy and light in the flower? What colour does the smell suggest? Does the colour suggest a sweet smell or a sour? Is the feel of the flower the same as the colour of the flower? Is there more of one colour than another? How would you like to show that these colours can grow on the paper (1)? Would you put the heavy colours or the light colours down first (2)? Did you find heavy and light colours? Where in your paper will you arrange them? Would the heavy colours be at the top or the bottom? Why?

Arrange the colours so as to make your eye move from one side of the page to the other. What colours move in and out (3)? (Warm and cold.) Will you use opaque or transparent colours (4)? If you use tissue paper how will you make the colour opaque? (By overlapping.) Select the colours that match the colours in the flowers.

EVALUATION: How many got a happy mood in their painting (5)? Who thinks that the colours they used suggest the smell of the flowers? Do the colours merge together or do they stand out against each other (6)? How many people were able to mix and match the colours to the flowers? How many yellows, blues, green and reds did you find? Were they all the same weight (7)?

EXPANDING OPPORTUNITIES: To use many variations of the one colour in a painting.

LEARNING SITUATION: Relating colour to mood, depicting the different characteristics of personalities

PROCESS: Painting with free brush work

MATERIALS: Tempera paint, newsprint, large brushes, containers for water, protection for desks and cleaning-up equipment

LEARNING:

1. Expressing quality of colour
2. Stating the problem
3. Terminology (Portrait   — Profile

MOTIVATION: I am sure you all have a friend or a relative whom you admire very much. Could you tell in words what is special about this person? Is this person sad, happy or funny? What would we call this? (Moods.) What colour would you use to show happiness? What colour would you use for sadness (1)?

Today we are going to show the mood of a person with colour (2). You may pick an imaginary person and paint a portrait of him or her. This portrait of the person may show any mood you like. Think what mood you will paint. Will you show the front face or profile (3)? Do not forget to fill the paper.

EVALUATION: What type of person does your portrait show? Do the colours tell about the kind of person? What kind of colours show us a happy person? What kind of person would we show with dark, drab colours? Do we know what the warm colours are? What are the cold colours? How do cold colours make you feel? Did you put anything else in the portrait of the person to show the mood? I hope you filled the space.

EXPANDING OPPORTUNITIES: Pupils may depict many interpretations of various personalities: 'The frightening witch', 'The monster', 'The happy clown'.

LEARNING SITUATION: Introducing the process of stencilling, showing the relationship between figure and ground

PROCESS: Stencilling, using cut or torn paper shapes

MATERIALS: Newsprint, tempera with paste added, short-haired brushes (tooth-brushes, stencil brushes or any worn brush), containers for paint, cleaning-up equipment

LEARNING:

1. Stating the problem
2. Process — teacher demonstration
3. Figure and background positive and negative

MOTIVATION: I am sure you all remember doing printing before with potato blocks. Today we are going to do printing with stencils (1).

We will cut out the shape of a person, animal, bird or whatever you like. We will call this the stencil. Now place it down on the paper and dab all around the edge with colour (2). Consider the spaces around the stencil shapes as important. This is the part that will be printed, leaving the stencil shape as the background (3). Try and find exciting ways to place the stencil so as to get interesting background shapes.

EVALUATION: Who was able to get the background shapes to stand out clearly? What do we mean when we talk about the background? Who can give an example? What did we discover today? (The part we printed became the background.) What do we call the shape? (The figure.) So we discovered a figure and ground; could we reverse the way we did it? What would we have to do with the stencil? We would have to cut the figure out and use what remains as the stencil.

EXPANDING OPPORTUNITIES: Creating stencils from negative shapes.

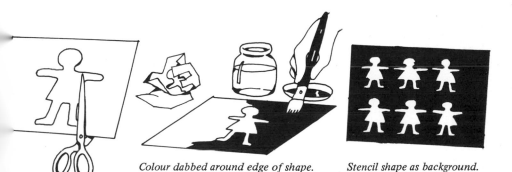

Colour dabbed around edge of shape.   *Stencil shape as background.*

Shape cut from paper.

LEARNING SITUATION: Expressing an idea through continuous linear organisation

PROCESS: Arranging string on card to use as a printing block

MATERIALS: Newsprint, crayons, heavy cord, cardboard in various sizes, adhesive, scissors, roller (Brayer), rolling slab (hard board)

LEARNING:

1. Process   3. Teacher demonstration
2. Stating the problem

MOTIVATION: Today we will make another kind of print (1). The block for this print will be cardboard and string. First we will try out some ideas with crayon on paper (2). The paper will have to be the same size as the block. So we will place the cardboard down on the paper and draw a line around the edge. In this rectangle now draw something you like but do not take the crayon off the paper when you draw. We call this a continuous line. Now we will transfer our continuous line drawing onto the cardboard (3). On the transferred lines we will put glue. Then stick the string to them. This will be your new printing block. Check that the spaces between the lines are not too wide, otherwise the background will pick up the paint. Now roll the paint on the block and you are ready for printing. We now place the paper for printing over the block leaving a margin all around and cover it with old newspaper. You now press it gently with your hand or a dry roller and you have the print.

EVALUATION: Who was able to get a clean print? (No paint in the background.) Do the lines show a continuous effect? Where else would you see lines like these? (Shells, pottery.) Do we know any painting that has continuous line in it?

EXPANDING OPPORTUNITIES: Continuous lines discovered in nature may be used to create a new block using polystyrine, meat trays and continuous line.

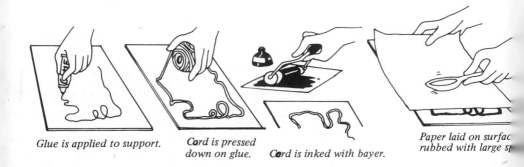

Glue is applied to support.   *Card is pressed down on glue.*   *Card is inked with bayer.*   *Paper laid on surfac rubbed with large s*

LEARNING SITUATION: Creating images based on the sound

PROCESS: Tissue paper painting

MATERIALS: Assorted colour tissue paper, adhesive, cartridge paper, paper for support, scissors and crayons

LEARNING:

1. Recalling   3. Related shapes
2. Stating the problem   4. Symbol

MOTIVATION: Who can recall a sound that describes movement? Who can give examples? What would the sound of a lawn mower be like? — The sound of shattering glass, — a fast engine, — water pouring, — a gale?

I am sure you all will be able to remember a sound. We will describe this sound of movement with a large coloured shape and line using tissue paper and crayon. Maybe the shape will have smaller shapes within it (3). The materials are now distributed and pupils are asked to cut shapes and arrange them on cartridge (support) paper. Apply the adhesive to the cartridge paper — not to the tissue as the colour runs.

EVALUATION: Pupils are asked to hold up their paintings. Can we tell the sound from it? The different sounds may be discussed. How does the shape tell us the sound? (The contour line describes a movement.) Is it only the shape that tells us about the movement? No — the colour can tell us too. Who can name something else that tells us about a sound? (The letters of the alphabet, etc.) What would we call this? (A symbol) (4)

EXPANDING OPPORTUNITIES: Creating symbols to express speed.

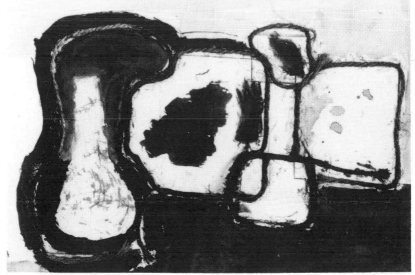

Drawing with string and colour.

LEARNING SITUATION: To create a picture expressing time and change (Story in frame form.)

PROCESS: Drawing

MATERIALS: Newsprint, tempera paint, brushes, jars of water, protection for desks etc.

LEARNING:

1. Recalling
2. Stating the problem

3. Process
4. Terminology

MOTIVATION: You remember the pictures we made of the way time changes wood (1). Today we are going to make a picture showing time and change. This picture will be like a comic strip (2). What is a comic strip? It is a number of frames (4) and each frame tells us a different part of the story. So we will arrange our story in a number of rectangles (3). The same person has to be in each frame. We will call this person Mr. Blue. All sorts of things happen to poor Mr. Blue in time. I am sure you will be able to tell all about them. Put your ideas in each frame using strong and effective lines and shapes to describe the picture parts.

Colour plays an important part. Maybe Mr. Blue meets a red dog or a pink panther in a green wood. Does everybody understand what is required? Make one rectangle at a time and you can join them all up afterwards. Paper cut in rectangles 15 x 10cm are distributed to each student and paints are also distributed. When you have one frame finished you can get another and remember something is happening to Mr. Blue in every one of the frames. When you have a number finished, we will paste them on a long strip so that we can fold them up in book form.

EVALUATION: Different pupils are asked to display their story of Mr. Blue and individual pupils in the class are asked to try and verbalise the story from the different frames. All work at a later stage is put on display.

EXPANDING OPPORTUNITIES: Historical events may be expressed in this manner.

LEARNING SITUATION: To discover the effect of light on a three-dimensional form

PROCESS: Constructing three-dimensional form and examining the effects of light on it

MATERIALS: Paper cartons all shapes, sizes and kinds, adhesive, scissors

LEARNING:

1. Teacher demonstration   2. Stating the problem

MOTIVATION: Who can tell what causes a shadow? (All forms with projection placed in light cast shadows) (1).

Today we are going to make light catchers (2). We will see how we will cut and join these boxes to make 'light catchers'. Find out the different ways you can cut and stick one into the other so that they will cast shadows.

EVALUATION: Now place your light catcher in the light and examine how it changes. How many different changes can you find by moving it? Where else would we find something like this? (In buildings.) Do you think when the Architect is designing the building, does he think of the effect of light on his work? (The sculpture.)

EXPANDING OPPORTUNITIES: Tracing the cast shadows on a sheet of white paper and creating a new form.

Shadows cast by forms.

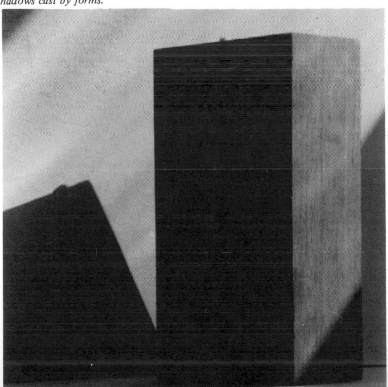

LEARNING SITUATION: Expressing emotions through facial expressions

PROCESS: Photo-montage

MATERIALS: A collection of large photographs of faces and hands from magazines, adhesive, scissors, grey sugar paper

LEARNING:

1. Vocabulary   3. Terminology
2. Stating the problem   4. Relating

MOTIVATION: Sometimes we can say things with our faces. We do not have to use words. Who can give an example? We call this facial expression (1). What sort of facial expression can we find? (Happy, sad, cross, surprised, sorry, puzzled, furious, thoughtful.)

Magazines are now distributed and pupils are asked to cut a large head or hands and paste it on the grey paper so that it fills up the paper (2). They are now asked to change the facial expression with different eyes, eyebrows, lips, etc. cut from other photographs. When they are satisfied with the new facial expression they are asked to paste the parts down.

We call what we did a photo-montage.

EVALUATION: Individual photo-montages are held up and the class is asked to identify the facial expressions. Where do we see facial expressions used? (In mime, television, posters and in drama) (4). What other way can we show how we feel through the human figure?

EXPANDING OPPORTUNITIES: Expressing the human figure under different emotional circumstances.

LEARNING SITUATION: Discovering the necessity of symbols as a quick way of reading

PROCESS: Cutting and sticking shapes

MATERIALS: Construction card, assorted coloured paper, adhesive, scissors

LEARNING:

1. Vocabulary   3. Relating
2. Stating the problem

MOTIVATION: Cut large shapes that denote common traffic signs from coloured construction card, or have a poster of traffic control symbols. The class is asked to read these signs.

What do we call these? We call them traffic symbols (1). What do symbols do for us? They tell us messages quickly (rapid communication).

Construction card, coloured paper and scissors are distributed to each pupil and they are asked to make a new symbol without words, which would indicate 'Stop', 'turn right', 'hills', 'bumpy road', 'tree down'. Select one you like best or think of some more (2).

EVALUATION: Individual pupils are asked to display their designs and the class is asked to identify them. What must a good symbol have? (It must be easy to read.) What else? (Shapes clearly defined.) Discuss briefly how man designed symbols in the past? (A few visuals would help.) What would you say was the first symbol for pointing the direction? (Finger or arrow.)

EXPANDING OPPORTUNITIES: Colour can have many meanings.

FOURTH CLASS

Art Growth Characteristics

1. Mixed work; schema alongside realistic representation
2. Experiences are described in a direct manner.
3. The profile is being added to the figure.
4. Beginning to understand foreshortening and overlapping.
5. Knows the difference between objects in nature and his own schematic drawing.
6. Landscapes are being attempted.
7. Very interested in manipulative experiences, i.e. refinement in handling tools and media.
8. Perceives more detail with greater accuracy.
9. Discovers he can represent objects more related to visual realism.
10. Strongly social.
11. Likes to excel in something.
12. Interested in colour variations, shades, intensities, forms, size and function.

Behavioural Objectives (Intended outcome for the pupil)

Pupils will be able to:
    Express movement found in nature
    Express rhythm three-dimensionally
    Understand shape as meaning and function
    Develop a symbol
    Construct from planes
    Understand the significance of the quality of line
    Create a visual expression of the environment
    Paint rhythm from music
    Express the contrast found in nature
    Create imaginary landscapes
    Express in contour line
    Understand foreground, middle ground and background
    Understand colour balance
    Understand basic structure

Pupils will be able to manipulate media and tools:
    Drawing with various media — charcoal, brush, crayon, soft pencil, felt markers,
    Painting in tempera
    Collage
    Continuous line drawing
    Cardboard construction
    Lettering with different tools
    Tissue paper painting
    Line stamping
    Stencilling

FOURTH CLASS

Learning Situations:
1. To discover movement within something still.
2. Discovering movement within the environment and creating symbols through line to create it.
3. To describe shapes that achieve repetition and variation.
4. Examining rhythm in nature and using these rhythms to make mobiles (Shapes achieving movement).
5. Relating figure and ground; Discovering that plant shapes and textures can relate visually to denote a terrain.
6. Understanding shape as meaning — relationship of function and shape.
7. To develop a symbol for Christmas.
8. To express an idea through textural surfaces.
9. Discovering form and construction from planes.
10. Discovering that line, an art element, can be a symbol for the edge of a form.
11. Discovering that the quality of lines themselves can be significant.
12. Creating a visual expression of environment making use of 'stuck-on' textures and pattern.
13. Discovering that rhythm found in music can be expressed through painting.
14. Creating pictures that show feelings.
15. Discovering contrasts and variety in nature and expressing it through shape, colour and texture.
16. Creating new forms by destroying forms.
17. Creating an imaginary landscape of rock forms.
18. Contour line drawing.
19. Developing foreground, middle ground and background.
20. Discovering different colours and tone in a form.
21. Developing an understanding of colour balance.
22. Discovering the basic structure of a natural form.
23. Creating a repeat pattern using a stencil shape.
24. Discovering lettering styles and creating new letters.

LEARNING SITUATION: To discover movement within something 'still'

PROCESS: Wax resist with crayon and diluted tempera paint

MATERIALS: Crayons, tempera paint, cartridge paper

LEARNING: Perceiving

1. Change of position
2. Movement within a fixed position
3. Body movement
4. Lateral and longitudinal movement
5. Free movement
6. Stating the problem
7. Teacher demonstration
8. Creating a new form with inner and outer dynamic lines

MOTIVATION: Would anybody like to say what movement is (1)? Can you move and yet stay in the one place (2)? Does a tree move? How? Can you show this with your body (3)? Does a stone move (4)? How does a fish move in a glass bowl (5)? Can you look for an object in the room and describe the movement within it?

Will you now express this movement with line on your sheet of paper remembering to show all the different types of movement you have found within your object (6). Remember to make the water-colour wash darker or lighter than the crayon lines (7).

When you have completed the 'wash', draw in the contour lines that the movement lines suggest. Make some of these inside lines touch the outer line (8). What does this new form suggest to you? Build up further lines and different colour washes to develop original forms.

EVALUATION: Does your form in your picture express movement? Does the body of a motor car suggest movement? Name other machines that express movement. In what way does the shape of the car change when it is actually moving?

EXPANDING OPPORTUNITIES: Discovering radiating lines, expanding lines, lines that create tension, converging and diverging movements.

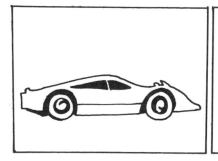
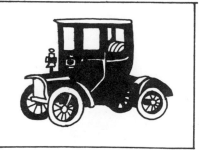

LEARNING SITUATION: Discovering movement in the environment and creating symbols through line to express it

PROCESS: Cutting and pasting

MATERIALS: White cartridge paper, scissors and paste. Examples of traffic symbols

LEARNING:

1. Sign and language   3. Stating the problem
2. Produce visuals

MOTIVATION: When we wish to tell something quickly without using words what do we use? We use symbols. Ask the class for examples of symbols (2). What is the purpose of a symbol? (To enable us to understand something quickly without using words.) Could you cut strips of paper and arrange them to show movement, e.g. 'go slow', 'move quickly', 'turn fast', 'change lanes' (3)? When you have arranged these strips to your satisfaction paste them down, not forgetting to make your symbol as large as possible.

EVALUATION: Arrange the symbols around the room. Can we all read these symbols? Or is it good if only the person who made them can read them? Does simplicity help us to read the symbol more clearly? Can we view small symbols from a distance?

EXPANDING OPPORTUNITIES: Search for unintentional symbols in objects and express them through line.

LEARNING SITUATION: To describe shapes that achieve repetition and variation

PROCESS: Cutting and arranging gummed coloured shapes

MATERIALS: Gummed coloured paper, support, scissors

LEARNING: Perceiving

1. Continuity   2. Stating the problem

MOTIVATION *(Visual and Verbal)*: Would you like to make a comic strip? Why do we like comic strips? Is it the story they tell? Is it because of the colour pictures? Is it because of the characters? Do we find the same character repeated in each picture? Why? It helps us to move from one rectangle to the next (1). Besides the principal character do we usually find other characters?

In our comic strip we will have a main character who appears in every rectangle throughout the story. First of all we will have to think of the shape and name of the principal character. He need not have a human shape. What story would you like to build about your character? Could it be about some 'fantastic journey' he is making? Tell all about a whole variety of wonderful shapes he meets along the way. The start of your story could show where your character is setting off from on his journey, then all the things that happen to him, ending with something exciting.

On your sheet of paper a number of rectangles should be drawn: as many as you think your story requires, and don't forget to make them the size 15 x 10cm (2). In these rectangles arrange the principal character so that he stands out, and replace the other shapes you think are necessary.

EVALUATION: How much of the rectangle did your principal character occupy? Does anyone find their principal character too small for the rectangle? Did you make sure that the principal shape is repeated in each? What makes the rectangles different? The same? (Repetition of main shapes, variation of secondary shapes.) Can we follow the story without words? Why?

LEARNING SITUATION: Examining rhythm in nature and using these rhythms to make mobiles (Shapes achieving movement.)

PROCESS: Cutting shapes for mobiles from stiff card, stringing and assembling these shapes in space; colour can be added

MATERIALS: Stiff card, string, tempera paints, scissors

LEARNING: Perceiving

1. The petals of the flowers, sounds in the room, foliage on the trees, books on the shelves, etc.

2. Stating the problem

MOTIVATION: What has rhythm got? It has repetition, that is, things which repeat with size, variation and space variation. Where do we find things that repeat in size? Where do we find things where the spaces between vary (1)?

Use the shapes that you have seen in nature to make a mobile (2). See that you arrange them so that they repeat when moving. (Use more than one of the same shapes.) String shapes and assemble mobile. Set it in motion.

EVALUATION: Can we see the spaces between the shapes? Are they changing and repeating? Are some close and some far apart? Do the shapes change in size and in colour, but remain the same shape?

EXPANDING OPPORTUNITIES: Design a block for printing using drawings from the mobiles of the in-between shapes. Paint these shapes to show repetition of a unit.

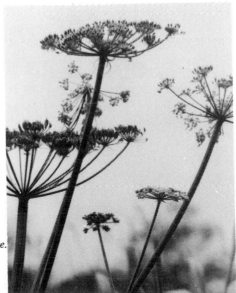

Rhythm in nature.

LEARNING SITUATION: Relating figure and ground; discovering that plant shapes and textures can relate visually to climate and terrain

PROCESS: Cutting shapes, relating lines and arrangement

MATERIALS: Two sheets of cartridge paper, tempera paint, brushes, jars for water, mixing dishes, protection for desks, cleaning-up materials

LEARNING:

1. Stating the problem
2. Background
3. Related colour and line
4. Contrast
5. Structures relate to supply of materials

MOTIVATION: Cacti or other small plants may be used as a visual source. What country does the cactus plant come from? What sort of climate has it got? Why do you think the shape is like that? What does the plant tell us? (The shape protects it from the sun; the projecting parts give it shade.) Look at all the shapes you can find in the plant, draw these shapes, then paint them, cut them out and arrange them on your second sheet of paper (1). This is their environment. Have we an art term for this (2). What must you do with this environment or background (3)? You can relate lines and shapes. What does related mean? (If there are curved lines in the first shapes we will have curved lines in the background. They will be the same but different.) What hues will you use, warm or cold? Think about the climate and your cactus shapes.

EVALUATION: Work is displayed. Let us see if we have different environments. Who succeeded in relating lines, shapes and colours? How many thought of dark and light? What else did we have to think of (4)? (Big and small.) Are houses related to the environment? Why were houses built in stone in some parts of the country and timber in other parts (5)? Could a part of a building tell us about the character of the entire building? Windows can tell us a lot. What about roofs? Are the roofs of the houses in Switzerland and North Africa the same? Why not? (One is built for cold weather and snow and the other for the hot weather.)

EXPANDING OPPORTUNITIES: Looking at street furniture; discovering the different shapes and lines and how they are related to place and time. (Street lamps, railings, seating, litter bins, flower containers, etc.)

LEARNING SITUATION: Understanding shape as meaning; relationship of function and shape

PROCESS: Cutting and shaping

MATERIALS: Scissors, tinfoil trays

LEARNING: Perceiving

1. Perceiving
2. Shape relation to function
3. Stating the problem

4. Decoration as function
5. Plastic forms are made from moulds

MOTIVATION: Ask pupils to bring a spoon, a knife and a fork. Place them on a viewing stand, group the ones that are similar. Ask the pupils to look at them as if they had never seen spoons, knives and forks before (1). Question pupils: Why is the shape of the spoon different from that of the knife or fork? Would the shape of the spoon tell you what it is for? (Focus on the different-shaped spoons and their different functions) (2). Can a fork have a similar function to a spoon? (The tulip-shaped fork can. It can scoop up.) Tinfoil trays and scissors are distributed and pupils are asked to make a spoon of their own design (3).

EVALUATION: Does your spoon tell us its function? Are parts of the shape related more to decoration or function (4)? Is the part you grip related to your hand? Who could give me an example where the handle is related to the hand? Are there places for your fingers in the new plastic handles (5)?

EXPANDING OPPORTUNITIES: Discovering that decoration can be an integral part of a form.

LEARNING SITUATION: To develop a symbol for Christmas

PROCESS: Cutting, arranging and pasting

MATERIALS: Coloured paper, paper for support, scissors, paste, old newspapers for covering desks

LEARNING:

1. Stating the problem
2. Christmas greeting cards
3. The lighted candle, the star in the east, the Magi, etc.
4. The emotional content

MOTIVATION: We all know what a symbol is. It is a quick way of giving a message. Who can give an example of one?

Today we are going to design a symbol for Christmas (1). Where would you find symbols for Christmas (2)? What are they like (3)? Are these good symbols? Do you think there is too much of a sameness about them? What is the meaning of Christmas? How could it be pictured? How do we feel about it (4)? What would be the best way to show it in shapes and colour?

Try and invent a new symbol for Christmas. Coloured paper, paste and scissors are now distributed.

EVALUATION: Work is put on display and pupils are asked to talk about their symbols. Why did you use that particular colour and shape? Is the arrangement related to the sheet of paper? Did we make good use of the empty space? How many expressed it as a joyous occasion? Commercial Christmas cards may be displayed and discussed.

EXPANDING OPPORTUNITIES: Further symbols may be created for other holidays.

'The Gate.' Painted textures.

LEARNING SITUATION: To express an idea through textural surfaces

PROCESS: Selecting, shaping, arranging and pasting

MATERIALS: Support paper (cartridge), pages from discarded pictorial magazines, scissors, paste, bags for waste paper

LEARNING:

1. Textures
2. Contrast

3. Procedure
4. Pottery, wall covering, furniture

MOTIVATION: Magazines are distributed and pupils are asked to find photographs that contain surfaces they can almost feel? What do we call these surfaces (1)? Do we notice any differences in textures (2)? Pupils may name the contrasts. Pupils are asked to sort their textures according to smooth and rough and characteristics, also dark and light. These textures may suggest a subject to you, but you must make your own shapes, not the shape in the photograph. If you are making a head you might use the texture of straw for the hair or grass. Do you all understand what to do (3)? You change the textures around. Allow some of the background to show through.

EVALUATION: Pupils display their work. Did we find that some textures are similar? We were able to show clouds with cotton wool, wire for hair. Did we find that a crowd became texture? The branches of the trees became texture. Was anybody able to use the bark of the tree for the texture of an elephant? How do we use texture in our environment? Can it be used for decoration? Where do you find it used as decoration (4)? Is it important to us? Do artists use texture?

EXPANDING OPPORTUNITIES: Relating textures to shapes, creating textures.

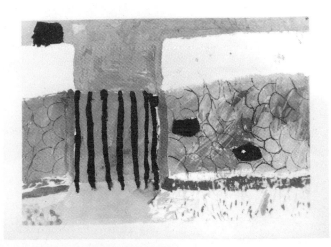

LEARNING SITUATION: Discovering form and construction from planes

PROCESS: Arranging and slotting planes of cardboard

MATERIALS: Scissors, cardboard (from shirt boxes, cornflake boxes, etc.), tempera paint, brushes, jars for water, protection for desks, cleaning-up material

LEARNING:

1. A volume (art terminology)
2. It may be a cup, a pencil, a sculpture, a motor car
3. Stating the problem
4. A box
5. Teacher demonstration

MOTIVATION: Today we are going to create a form (1). Who knows what a form is? It is an art term. A form is three-dimensional. You can walk around it. Who would like to give me an example of a form (2). You will build this form by adding these rectangles together (3). The cardboard rectangles are now distributed. We will call these planes. What else has planes (4)? Our problem is to join these planes without using glue or tape so that we will make a form that will stand by itself. It can be done by cutting slots in each rectangle and joining them by slipping one into the other (5). See if you can make a form that is as wide as it is high. The form may be painted when it is completed.

EVALUATION: Let us see who was able to get the form to stand. Does your form represent anything? What do we call a form that does not represent anything? (Non-objective.) What does an art form like sculpture share with music? (Time, as one has to walk around and see, rather than hear, different parts before going on to the next.)

EXPANDING OPPORTUNITIES: Discovering the play of light and shadow on the various planes.

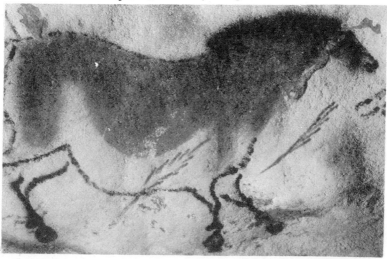

LEARNING SITUATION: Discovering that line, an art element, can be a symbol for the edge of a form

PROCESS: Drawing with a continuous line

MATERIALS: Newsprint, soft pencil, charcoal or felt markers, weathered stones

MOTIVATION: Stones, paper and pencils are distributed to each student. We will call this stone a form. See if you can describe this form with a continuous line. When you commence drawing do not lift the pencil or stop until you have completed the form. When each pupil has the drawing completed they are questioned. What do you see on the paper? What do you read from it? Some pupils may answer — a stone; others may say a line. Pupils are asked to turn the stone and see if they can find other edges and describe them also in line. When they have a number of edges drawn, a new sheet of paper is distributed. Pupils are asked to look at their drawing and pick out the line that best describes the stone and draw it on the new sheet. When this is completed, pupils are questioned. Is there anything missing? Look again at the stone. Yes there are lines in the inside. These interior lines are necessary to give a better description of the form. Pupils are asked to look at and draw these lines.

EVALUATION: Pupils' work is displayed. Who can tell what they discovered when they were drawing the form? Was the single continuous line enough to describe the form? What did it describe for us? (An edge.) How many edges did you discover? Has the form other lines? (Interior lines which describe new edges.) To describe the form accurately, we must consider all the lines within it. If we are drawing the figure, what would we look for? Do you think line is an invention? Who knows when man started using line? (Refer to Lascaux Caves in France.)

EXPANDING OPPORTUNITIES: Further natural form may be examined and drawn in line to discover the message within it. (The descriptive content.)

Using line 20,000 years ago. Horse from the Lascaux Caves.

LEARNING SITUATION: Discovering that the quality of lines themselves can be significant

PROCESS: Drawing lines using the edges of pieces of cardboard for stamping

MATERIALS: Newsprint, cardboard, tempera paint, paper pads, dishes, (brushes may also be used)

LEARNING:

1. Stating the problem
2. Teacher demonstration
3. Creativeness
4. The mark of the tool as a stimulus
5. Decorative line

MOTIVATION: The last day we found we could describe a form by the lines which are without and within it. Today we are going to use lines which we shall invent and make them important (1).

A piece of cardboard about 7 x 10cm is cut so that it has one long side, a shorter one, a shorter one still and a very short side. Teacher demonstrates how to use by pressing the edges into thined tempera paint, or the paint may be dabbed on the edges with a brush (2). Paper is distributed and pupils are asked to practise a number of lines. When they have practised, a new sheet is distributed. They are now asked to create a form from their imagination (3). If they have to use curves these must be made by using a number of short lines which give the illusion of a curve. The form may develop from the lines.

EVALUATION: Work is displayed. Who found that the lines suggested a form (4)? Did you think of a form before you started? Who related the form to the sheet of paper? Did anybody show movement? Describe your drawing? Did we find that the arrangement of the lines was most important? Do you think artists use lines that are not found in objects? Where else would you find lines that are seen in objects? (Decoration — symbols — abstract art) (5). So we can use line for its own sake.

EXPANDING OPPORTUNITIES: To create a decoration using straight lines.

LEARNING SITUATION: Creating a visual expression of an environment; making use of 'stuck-on' textures and pattern

PROCESS: Collage

MATERIALS: A collection of 'actual' textures — sacking, different kinds of paper, cloth, carpets, sawdust, woodshavings, stones, corrugated cardboard, bus tickets, cord, twigs, shells, textures from magazine advertisements — PVA glue, scissors, stapler, cardboard for support

LEARNING:

1. Visual recall
2. Stating the problem
3. Contrast
4. Variation
5. Art element

MOTIVATION: Who can think of some place he was in that had a lot of textured surfaces (1)? Imagine you put all the textures together, would these textures tell us something about the place? For example what textures would you find in a butcher's shop? Would there be any difference between it and the textures you would find in a park?, We will call these environments. Today we are going to create an environment with textures (2). Think out some environment and tell about it through a collage. Cardboard is distributed for a support. Some may use actual textures and others may use textures from magazines. Sometimes it is best if the edges are torn rather than cut. Thread can be pulled from sacking or cloth to give a better effect. Do not forget to cover most of the format (cardboard support). To give the eye a rest we might leave some parts blank (3). Try and make the edges of the spaces different sizes (4).

EVALUATION: Work is displayed and pupils are questioned. Who can tell what environment that is? (Answer is verified by owner.) Who made sure to leave background spaces empty? What effect has that on the collage? (It emphasises the different textures, otherwise it would be 'too busy'.) How important is texture (5)? What would it be like if we had no texture? Did artists always use texture? Who do you think was one of the first artists to use the word *collage*? (Pablo Picasso.) Who was Pablo Picasso?

EXPANDING OPPORTUNITIES: Creating textures with marks from different tools (cord, twigs, sponges, feathers, etc.) and expressing 'The City', 'The Country', 'The Jungle'.

LEARNING SITUATION: Discovering that rhythm found in music can be expressed through painting

PROCESS: Painting

MATERIALS: Newsprint, tempera colour, brushes, containers for water, mixing dishes, protection for desks

LEARNING:

1. Art elements   3. Sculpture
2. Stating the problem   4. Poetry

MOTIVATION: Pupils are asked to listen to the playing of a selected recording. When you are listening do you feel like moving your bodies? (The movement will depend on the kind of music selected — traditional, classical, jazz, marching or any other musical trend.) What made you move? Do you repeat similar movements? Do they repeat the same way (regular) or do they change? How do we keep time to the music? We will call this rhythm. Does all music have the same rhythm? In making a painting how would we put rhythm in it (1)? First, we might think of lines and see how they are repeated. Where would we find the lines? (Around the edges of shapes.) We could repeat straight lines and curved lines. We could repeat similar shapes. We could repeat the same colour, we also could repeat the same type of brush stroke.

Materials are distributed, a new recording is played and pupils are asked to paint a picture which will represent the music (2). Listen carefully and think of what colours you see, maybe these colours are repeated in large shapes and small shapes, straight lines and curved lines. Do not forget the different kinds of brush strokes.

EVALUATION: Work is displayed. Let us see if we can see the different rhythms in the painting. Individual pupils are questioned about their work. Why did you select that particular colour to repeat? Was it the instrument or the note that suggested that colour to you? How many found it was easier to show the rhythm with the brush stroke? Show the class two reproductions, one with a repetition of brush strokes and one with repetition of shapes. (Vincent Van Gogh, George Braque.) In what other ·art form would you find rhythm (3)? A short poem could be read and pupils could identify the rhythm made by the words.

EXPANDING OPPORTUNITIES: Creating images from poetry (4).

Opposite: 'At the dentist.' Expressing feelings and emotions.

LEARNING SITUATION: Creating pictures that show feelings

PROCESS: Painting

MATERIALS: Tempera paint, brushes, newsprint, containers for water, mixing dishes, protection for desks

LEARNING:

1. Expressing posture
2. Pupils own reaction
3. Verbalise their reactions to the painting

MOTIVATION: If you were sad, how do you think you would stand? Who would like to show me? If you were happy would you stand in a different way? What are we doing? We are showing our feelings in the way we stand (1). We could also show these feelings on paper with paint and brush. I am sure you all would like to paint a picture telling how you feel. We will pick these subjects – the wind, the sound of the traffic, flowers in summer. Select one of these and think carefully what colours would best express it. Materials are distributed. Remember you are showing how you feel (2). Make sure your picture fills the paper.

EVALUATION: Work is displayed. Can we see from these paintings how the persons who painted them felt? Pupils are asked to identify the different feelings in the paintings. Verify the correctness of the feelings with the owners. Show the class reproductions of some expressionist painters. (Vincent Van Gogh's 'Starry Night', Emil Noldes's woodcut 'The Prophet', Paul Gauguin's Self-Portrait.) Define this type of painting as 'expressionism'. Ask the pupils to feel the paintings and discuss their reactions (3). Direct their attention to the exaggeration of colour.

EXPANDING OPPORTUNITIES: Pupils may use various subject matter from their own experiences and create 'expressionist' paintings.

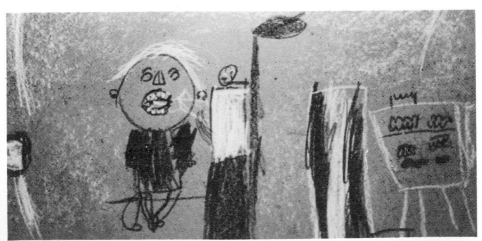

LEARNING SITUATION: Discovering contrasts and variety in nature and expressing them through shape, colour and texture

PROCESS: Drawing and cutting, painting and arranging

MATERIALS: Tempera paint, brushes, containers for water, mixing dishes, protection for desks, two sheets of newsprint, scissors, paste

LEARNING:

1. Visual recall
2. Statement of problem
3. Procedure
4. Imaginative use of shapes
5. Art terminology — counter change

MOTIVATION: As you have discovered there are many different contrasts (1). Who would like to name some for me? Who has seen a draught board or a chess board? Has it got contrast? (Black squares, White squares.) It has contrast, but has it got variety? What is variety? If you were eating the same food every day would you have variety?

Today we are going to look at different contrasts in our surroundings, contrasts of colour, of size, of shape, and texture. We may also find curved lines and straight lines. What are the two biggest contrasts (2)? The floor and the wall. What do we call them? The vertical and the horizontal planes. The horizontal or flat ground and the verticality of all that grows on it. The first sheet of paper is distributed and materials are distributed (3).

Look around you — when you have found a variety of contrasting shapes, draw them with the brush using a light colour. Now cut them out. The second sheet of paper is now distributed. Draw a line across the sheet of paper which will show the ground space and the sky space. Arrange the cut out, contrasting shapes so that they stand on the ground space. Maybe some will go up into the sky space. When you are satisfied with your arrangement paste them down. Now paint them making some dark and some light to show contrast. We might also use contrast of colour and texture (4).

EVALUATION: Work is placed on display. We will look now and see who was able to show contrast and variety. How many were able to make the shapes stand out against the ground space and the sky space? What had you to do to the shape when it went up into the sky space? (Dark against the sky, light against the ground or the reverse) (5). Look at the branches of the trees when they are seen against the sky, are they dark or light? Are the buildings dark or light when they rise up against the sky. What other contrasts can we find in nature? The soft foliage against the rectangular building. The soft clouds and the sharp branches of the trees. The bright yellow flower against the concrete.

EXPANDING OPPORTUNITIES: Creating a repeat pattern using contrasting shapes of various sizes.

Expressing space. Age: 9.

LEARNING SITUATION: Creating new forms by destroying forms

PROCESS: Cutting, arranging, pasting

MATERIALS: Photographs from magazines, newsprint (for support), paste, scissors, paints, brushes

LEARNING:

1. Vocabulary
2. Stating the problem
3. Art terminology
4. Relating shapes to the background
5. Understanding photo-montage

MOTIVATION: When we wish to make a chair what do we have to do to the tree? We have to cut down the tree, saw it into planks of wood, transform it (1). Today we will transform photographs (2). We call this a photo-montage (3). We will cut them so that we will have different parts. These parts will be rearranged to make something different. Photographs, paste, scissors and paper for support are now distributed. See if you can create something interesting by changing the parts. Fill up the page with your arrangement (4). You may add lines to the background.

EVALUATION: Work is put on display. Let us see if everybody was able to fill the paper. Who found interesting shapes in the background? Individual pupils are asked to talk about their painting. What sort of artist uses photo-montages (5)? (A graphic artist.) What is a graphic artist? (An artist who creates drawings for print.)

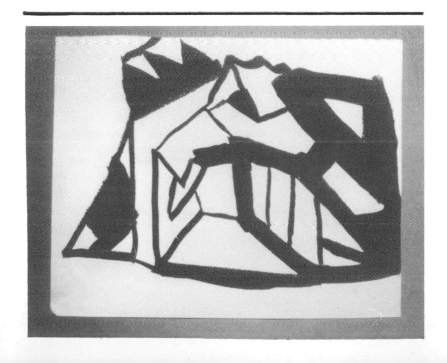

LEARNING SITUATION: Creating an imaginary landscape with rock forms

PROCESS: Drawing and painting

MATERIALS: Tempera paint, brushes, paper, containers for water, mixing dishes, protection for desks, stones, charcoal, scissors and paste

LEARNING:

1. Stating the problem
2. Outline drawing
3. Horizon
4. Contrast
5. Principle of design

MOTIVATION: Who would like to tell about the different types of landscape found in this country? (Mountain landscape, woodland, seascape, etc.)

Today we are going to create an imaginary landscape. We will call it a rock landscape (1). Paper, charcoal and a stone are distributed to each pupil. They are asked to look hard at the stone and see how many shapes they can find by turning it. Now draw these shapes on the sheet of paper (2). When they have completed the preliminary drawing they are given a new sheet of paper. Imagine this sheet of paper as a landscape, draw a line across it to show where the land and the sky meet (3). Now cut out the rock shapes you have and see if you can arrange them on your landscape so that they 'look good'. You will have different sizes. Arrange them in proportion so that you will give the feeling of distance. When you are satisfied with your arrangement paste down the shapes. Now you may paint them. If you like you may paint clouds in the sky. Are clouds the same shapes as rocks (4)?

EVALUATION: Work is put on display. Who was able to get some of the shapes going up into the sky? Was everybody able to get distance in their landscape? What way can we show distance? (By making the objects that are near big and those that are far small, by overlapping shapes, etc.) Some reproductions may be used to illustrate this. Who was able to get unity in their landscape (5)? We get unity when everything adds up to a unified whole that is the colour, shapes, and lines. What sort of a landscape have we around the school? How could we improve it? The Italian painter Andrea Mantegna (1431–1506) is supposed to have said: 'If you wish to paint a landscape go find yourself a rock.'

EXPANDING OPPORTUNITIES: Creating a city landscape.

LEARNING SITUATION: Contour line drawing

PROCESS: Drawing

MATERIALS: Charcoal, soft pencils, crayon or felt markers

LEARNING:

1. Stating the problem   3. Three-dimensional
2. Dark and light pattern

MOTIVATION: We are going to do contour line drawing today (1). What is contour line drawing? It is drawing done by looking and thinking that you are touching the object with the crayon.

Your eye is the crayon and both should move very slowly. Look only at the part your eye and crayon is on. It is not good to let your eye get ahead of the crayon. Remember to think you are touching the object. Do not look at the paper as you draw. You will have lines going in and out as well as lines that go up and down. You may look at your drawing when you stop. When you begin to draw again look back at the object and start at the same point as you left off.

Paper is distributed. Pupils are asked to take one shoe off, place it on the desk and draw it. When one drawing is completed pupils are asked to change the viewpoint and do another drawing.

Pupils may like to draw different views or different parts of the shoe, letting each contour overlap. They may then like to darken in some areas (2).

EVALUATION: Work is put on display. What did you discover when you were doing this type of drawing? Did you find that the edge did not end on the outline, but moved inside out? What else did you find? Does contour line drawing give a feeling of depth? What do we call this (3)? Pupils may be shown reproductions of line drawings by Matisse, Cezanne, Van Gogh. Their similarities and differences may be discussed.

EXPANDING OPPORTUNITIES: Making contour line drawing of plant forms.

LEARNING SITUATION: Developing foreground, middle ground and background

PROCESS: Drawing and painting

MATERIALS: Pencil, tempera paint, container for water, brushes, mixing dishes, paper

LEARNING:

1. Stating the problem
2. Perspective
3. More detail in near objects
4. Atmosphere blues the objects

MOTIVATION: Today we are going to think about space (1). We will create an imaginary room showing space. We will show objects in this room. Some will be near, we call this the foreground. Some will be further away, we call this the middle ground. Some will be far away, we call this the background or distance. Think carefully about this space. What will you put in the foreground, the middle ground and the background? Where will your viewpoint be, high up or low down? Are you looking down on the objects or up at them? Will the objects in the foreground be bigger than the objects in the background (2)? Will you have objects overlapping? If you look at this room it might help you to work out your idea.

Materials are distributed and pupils are asked to paint 'The Imaginary Room'.

EVALUATION: Work is placed on display. Let us see who was able to show space. What difference in detail do we see in objects that are near and objects that are far away (3)? Who put more detail in the foreground? Does the colour of objects change when they are in the distance (4)? Pupils may be shown reproductions of paintings which emphasise perspective.

EXPANDING OPPORTUNITIES: 'Walking in outer space'.

LEARNING SITUATION: Discovering different colours and tones in a form

PROCESS: Painting in tempera colour

MATERIALS: Tempera colour, cartridge paper, brushes, mixing dishes, dishes for containing colour (egg cartons), jars for water, small stones

LEARNING:

1. Stating the problem
2. The dark and light of the colour
3. Contrast

MOTIVATION: Distribute small stones. Pupils are asked if they can see variations of one colour or different colours. Are some lighter than others, are some darker than others? How can you be sure? If you squint your eyes you will see which is the darkest. Paints and paper are now distributed. Pupils are asked to see if they can make some colours lighter by adding white and darker by adding black. When they have experimented they can now see if they can match the colours on the stones (1). They can see how many colours and darks and lights they can match.

EVALUATION: Work is placed on display. Who found that some stones contained one colour but different tones? What does tone mean (2)? Why must we place a dark tone alongside a light tone (3)? Are there variations of tones in the sky or is the sky all the one colour? What colour is the sky today?

EXPANDING OPPORTUNITIES: Discovering the different tones of grey in the sky. Inventing a cold sky or a warm sky.

LEARNING SITUATION: Developing an understanding of colour balance

PROCESS: Tissue paper painting

MATERIALS: Assorted coloured tissue paper, white paper for support, PVA adhesive, strips of cardboard for applying adhesive

LEARNING:

1. Stating the problem
2. The blue is too heavy for the yellow
3. Teacher demonstration
4. Large amounts of a light colour to balance with small amount heavy colour

MOTIVATION: Today we are going to create a colour balance using tissue paper (1). If you had a large amount of blue and a small amount of yellow, would you have a colour balance? Why would you not have a balance (2)? We would have to have a large amount of yellow and a small amount of blue. Who can give me an example of a colour balance. Five colours are distributed to each pupil and paper for support, also adhesive and an adhesive spreader. Tear the tissue paper into various sizes and arrange them on the white paper (no white showing); the shape of colour need not represent anthing. When you have created a balance, lift up one piece of tissue at a time and apply the adhesive to the white paper and press the tissue paper down (3). (When the adhesive is applied to the tissue paper first the colour may run.) Continue pasting down until you have all the white paper covered. You may overlap some colours.

EVALUATION: Work is placed on display. Was everybody able to create a balance? What did you find (4)? What are the heavy colours? (Dark blue, black, dark brown, dark green, dark red, etc.) If a man had a blue suit what colour tie would he use to create a balance? What colour cardigan would a girl wear with a red dress? What colour cushion would you place with a green carpet? Reproductions may be examined for their colour balance?

EXPANDING OPPORTUNITIES: Discovering colour dominance.

LEARNING SITUATION: Discovering the basic structure of a natural form

PROCESS: Sgraffito (Crayon etching)

MATERIALS: Cartridge paper, assorted coloured crayons, nail files, cocktail sticks or oval wire nails

LEARNING:

1. Stating the problem
2. Terminology
3. The centre axis
4. Developing creativeness

MOTIVATION: Leaves or flowers or shells are distributed to each pupil. We are going to find the structure of the form you have (1). What does the word structure mean (2)? Who can give me an example of structure? (The arrangement of the parts.) What geometric shapes do you think they will fit into? A square, a rectangle, a triangle, a circle?

Draw a line first that shows the centre and consider the related geometric shape (3). Now draw other lines that show how the structure fits into that shape. When you have found the structure lines of one form try another one. More paper is distributed. Now see if you can create structure for a new form from your imagination (4).

EVALUATION: Work is put on display. How many were able to invent a new form? Maybe some invented new types of leaves. Did you make your outside lines relate to the structure lines? How do you think structure helps the design? Is it an important part? What part does structure play in the finished building? In what other art form do we use the word structure?

EXPANDING OPPORTUNITIES: Discovering lines that move over the form and across the surface to show the roundness.

LEARNING SITUATION: Creating a repeat pattern using a stencil shape

PROCESS: Stencil printing

MATERIALS: Stencilling or stiff card, one sheet of cartridge paper, one sheet of non-porous paper, scissors, thick liquid, tempera colour, dishes for colour, stiff bristled brushes or stencil brushes

LEARNING:

1. Stating the problem
2. Teacher demonstration
3. Background shape
4. A flow to the design

MOTIVATION: Today we are going to design a decorative cover for a book or wrapping paper (1). What sort of design do you usually find on wrapping paper? A repeat pattern. You all know what a repeat pattern is. (A repetition of a unit.) Our unit today will be a stencil shape. A shape is cut from the stiff card (construction paper) and placed on the top left of the cartridge paper. The paint is dabbed around the edge taking care that the paint does not 'bleed' under the stencil (2). When the stencil shape is again placed on the cartridge paper make sure to keep it as near as possible to the last shape so as to form a new shape between the two shapes (3). Continue in this manner until the whole paper is covered. Different colours can be applied to the one stencil or an overprint using a second stencil can be made after the first has dried. Such prints must be placed carefully to give a flow to the design.

EVALUATION: Prints are placed on display. Pupils are questioned. Who was able to discover new shapes between the stencil shapes? What was the best way to get a unified design? Does the eye move freely from one shape to the next? What do we call this? In what printing process is a stencil used? (Silkscreen.)

EXPANDING OPPORTUNITIES: Printing from cork or pieces of wood.

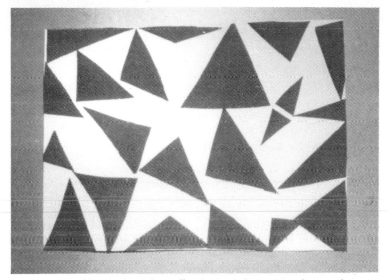

Pattern work. Repetition of shape. Emphasis on the positive shape and resultant negative shapes.

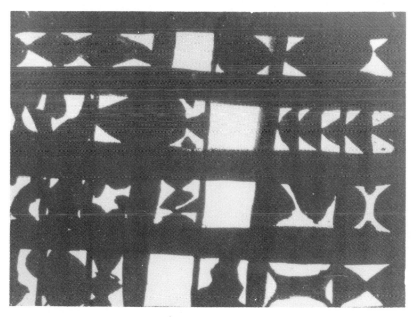

Pattern work. Expressing Variety/Unity. Design based on a grid of vertical and horizontal lines.

LEARNING SITUATION: Discovering lettering styles and creating new letters

PROCESS: Lettering with different tools

MATERIALS: Cartridge paper, newsprint, indian ink, ruler, timber from tomato chips cut into strips and tapered at one end to make various widths can be used as pens. Felt markers of various widths or pieces of cardboard held in clothes clips can also be used

LEARNING:

1. Stating the problem
2. Calligraphy
3. Printing

4. Capitals – lower case
5. Serifs – Sans Serif
6. The Romans

MOTIVATION: Pupils are required to bring in old magazines. They are questioned. How many are familiar with styles of lettering? Today we are going to find different styles of lettering (1). Some letters are made by hand and others are made by pressing the inked letter to the paper. Who knows what the first type of lettering is called (2)? And the second (3)? Pupils are asked to look through the magazines to see if they can find the two styles. Do you know what the big letters are called (4)? And the small letters (4)? Pupils are asked to study each letter carefully and compare the spaces in the upper part with the spaces in the lower part. Examine the open letters and the closed letters. (B, D, O, Q.) Pupils are asked to see if they can invent new letters by changing the sizes of the spaces in the letters. You may use guide lines (parallel) and these may be drawn lightly with the pencil and ruler. You can practise on newsprint first. Try the letters of your name. When you are satisfied with the letters, draw them on the cartridge paper making sure that they are related to the space – not too big or too small. Teacher may demonstrate how to use the different 'pens'.

EVALUATION: Work is put on display. Let us see who was able to invent a new style. Did you discover that some letters have little strokes at the ends of the lines? What are they called (5)? And the one without strokes (5)? Who were the first to use letters with serifs (6)?

EXPANDING OPPORTUNITIES: Discovering the slanting and vertical positions of letters, letters with double lines and split ends.

Ninivite Cuneiform (c. 3000 BC)

Egyptian Hieroglyphics (c. 3000)

ABCDEFGHIKLMabcdefghilmno 1234

Plantin Light

aбʋeғꙅhilmopрᴀбcʋeғꙅhlm 1234

Gaelic

ABCDEFGKLPQVWXZabcdefghilmn 12345

Baskerville

ABCDEFGHIKLMNabcdefghilm 123

Times

Round Hand Script

Chancery Letters

capitals and lower case. Capitals seven pen-widths high; lower case letters five pen-widths high and their ascenders and descenders each five pen-widths high.

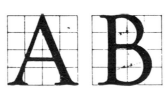

capitals above; lower case below.

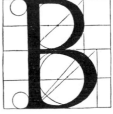

Sans Serif Letters capitals and lower case.

Roman Letters: formation of serif and body of letter.

See also page 193 for upper and lower case lettering.

FIFTH CLASS

Art Growth Characteristics

1. Emphasises contour lines of concrete objects.
2. Is becoming more analytical about his visual world.
3. Spontaneous drawing is declining.
4. Copying is on the increase.
5. Developing true-to-appearance representation from observation of pictures in books.
6. Dexterity with tools are developing into artistic expression.
7. Greater interest in longer working time.
8. Likes to establish his own interest areas.
9. Is representing figures and objects with greater three-dimensional accuracy.
10. Has better understanding of the relationship of objects.
11. Has a greater understanding of how to represent distance and space.
12. Is exhibiting efficiency in both two-dimensional and three-dimensional work.

Behavioural Objectives (Intended outcomes for the pupil)

Pupils will be able to:
    Understand unity and variety
    Understand dark and light structure
    Understand pattern in the environment
    Express tone through pencil
    Express form from observation
    Understand gesture drawing
    Understand design in everyday objects
    Understand spacing in lettering
    Understand the relationship of form to function
    Understand the emotional effect of colour
    Understand counterchange
    Create symbols

Pupils will be able to manipulate media and tools:
    Draw and shade with pencil
    Print from a relief block
    Paint with cardboard shapes
    Form in papier maché
    Model in plaster
    Tissue paper painting
    Collography
    Stabile construction
    Work in cut and torn paper

FIFTH CLASS

Learning Situations:

1. Discovering unity in variety.
2. To discover unity through line.
3. Creating a design to discover that shapes placed next to each other require contrast (light areas against dark areas).
4. Discovering pattern in the immediate environment of the school, inside and outside of the building. Making a mural to show how the patterns inside and outside are similar and different — discovering tactile and visual patterns.
5. Examining a form for tone and expressing it through pencil.
6. Drawing a self portrait, first using the sense of touch and then vision.
7. Expressing a figure through gesture drawing.
8. Expressing an idea through a relief print, making use of a previous drawing.
9. Creating a hand puppet, additive built up forms.
10. Expressing an idea with shapes and line and colour (cardboard stamping).
11. Discovering design in everyday objects.
12. Creating a relief panel to express pattern and rhythm.
13. Discovering pictorial composition.
14. Looking at motion as it occurs in nature (expressing a kinesthetic experience through a three-dimensional form).
15. Discovering that spacing in lettering helps the visual effect of words.
16. Designing a stage set or a diorama.
17. Creating an arrangement of textured shapes to express depth.
18. Designing a handle for a tool — discovering the relationship of the handle to the hand.
19. Expressing emotions and feelings through colour — the emotional effect of colour.
20. Discovering dark on light and light on dark (counterchange) — printing from cardboard.
21. Creating forms which express the balance of line against plane — lines which define shape.
22. Relating the human figure to shape.
23. Creating a symbol by working with cut or torn paper.
24. Drawing an object showing more than one side at a time.

LEARNING SITUATION: Discovering unity in variety

PROCESS: Printing with cardboard edge

MATERIALS: Paint, paper, strips of cardboard, dishes to hold paint

LEARNING: Perceiving

1. Monotony
2. Teacher role
3. Stating the problem
4. Size of square and linear marks
5. Different directions of the linear marks
6. Pattern

MOTIVATION: Without variety what have we got (1)? How would you feel if everything and everybody was the same? Do we like things to be different?

Distribute a sheet of paper to each pupil. Ask him to fold the sheet of paper into thirty-two equal squares. Distribute strips of cardboard cut to the width of the squares (2).

Dip edge of cardboard into the paint (one colour could be used) and stamp edge down on the paper support. Can you print three lines in each square to make a different arrangement each time (3)?

EVALUATION: Did everybody succeed in making each square different? What is common to each square (4)? What do you think makes the unity? What makes the variety (5)? How could we make greater variety and unity between the squares? Maybe you could extend the lines into other squares so that they meet. With the cardboard tool maybe you can make shorter and smaller clusters of dots and small lines. What would we call what we have done (6)?

EXPANDING OPPORTUNITIES: Discovering a pattern of line in buildings as a source for further pattern work.

LEARNING SITUATION: To discover unity through line

LEARNING: Perceiving

1. Unity
2. Common boundary

3. Continuous line
4. Overlapping and intersecting forms

MOTIVATION: Can you see a number of objects in the room that have different contours? In what way are these contours different? How could we unite them? Could we find an example of this in nature? (Example: Different people but one family.) How could we make one family of these different object contours (1)?

What we have to find is one thing that is common to them all. Could we say it is the sheet of paper that we put them on? Or, could we say it is the arrangement of them on the paper? Could you now arrange the contours of the objects on your sheets of paper and find out how you can unite them?

EVALUATION: How many found that there is a common line running through all the shapes? How many found two sides fitted together (2)? How many found that one edge flowed into the other (4)? Maybe you would like to add more lines which will help you to create a better unity.

EXPANDING OPPORTUNITIES: Discovering composite line in natural forms, where interrupted contours change the visual impact.

Pattern work. Vertical and horizontal lines common.

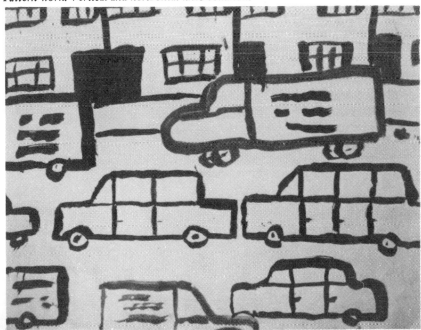

LEARNING SITUATION: Creating a design to discover that shapes placed next to each other require contrast (light areas against dark areas)

PROCESS: Cutting and tearing grey paper shapes, arranging and pasting down grey shapes on a white support. Drawing

MATERIALS: Grey sugar paper, white cartridge supports, paste and paste brushes, pencils, pentels, markers, charcoal, scissors

LEARNING: Perceiving

1. Stating the problem   2. Lack of contrast

MOTIVATION *(Direct Experience, Moving Towards Visual Experience)*: Distribute two sheets of paper, one grey and one white. Ask the pupils to use the white piece as a support and tear the grey piece into animal shapes. Pupils are then asked to arrange the grey animal shapes on the support, making sure to cover all the white spaces (1).

Pupils' attention could then be focused on the visual degrees of surface differences between the pasted down grey animal shapes.

Why do all the grey shapes look equally important in your arrangements (2)? What must we do with these shapes so that we can see them clearly? Pupils could be asked to give their understanding of contrast, e.g. black/white, day/night, high/low, front/back.

Look for dark and light areas in the room and draw these on a sheet of white paper. Paint in these shapes so that they contrast where they touch each other.

EVALUATION: Do the shapes surrounded by lighter and darker shapes have any effect on the original shapes? Why is contrast so important? What is the opposite to contrast?

EXPANDING OPPORTUNITIES: Paint a picture to show contrast, e.g. day and night. Add dark lines and light lines to the painting as a decorative enrichment of shape.

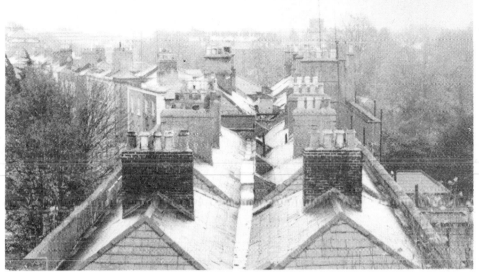

Shapes receding.

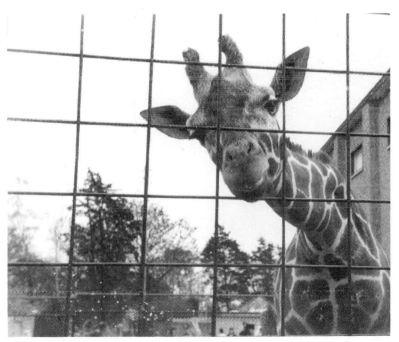

Shapes behind shapes.

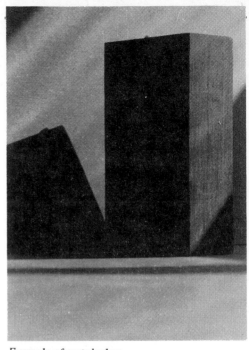

Example of cast shadow.

Pattern in the environment.

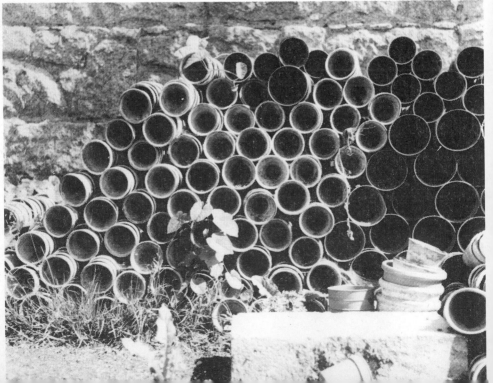

LEARNING SITUATION: Discovering pattern in the immediate environment of the school, inside and outside the building. Making a mural to show how the patterns inside and outside are similar and different. Discovering tactile pattern and visual pattern

PROCESS: Drawing and painting. Arranging, pasting, integrating

MATERIALS: Crayons and tempera paint, large sheets of brown paper or rolls of wallpaper to support individual patterns, a sheet of white paper for each student

LEARNING: Perceiving
(Patterns activity — contrasting light areas against dark areas in a composition.)

1. Units that are repeated to make larger units
2. No part of the support should be showing
3. Repetition and variety, shapes in winter and shapes in spring

MOTIVATION: Children are asked to look for shapes and surfaces that are different and alike in the immediate environment of school and to list these objects. Did you find that small objects are repeated to make bigger objects (1)? For example, bricks into a wall, walls into buildings, blades of grass making up a lawn, bars making up the railings, windows in the walls, slates in the roof, patterns in the pavement, furniture in the room.

Distribute a sheet of paper to each pupil and ask him to cover it with a pattern that he has individually observed (2). When individual patterns are completed, pupils are asked to assemble these patterns together in a large sheet of paper and paste them down to create a mural which expresses a story that integrates the patterns inside with the patterns outside.

EVALUATION: In what way are these patterns alike or unalike? Are the inside patterns different from the outside patterns? Can they be mixed? Why?

EXPANDING OPPORTUNITIES: Discovering that change depends on 'continuity' with differences.

LEARNING SITUATION: Examining a form for tone and expressing it through pencil

PROCESS: Pencil drawing

MATERIALS: Any variety of paper, smooth or textured, white or coloured, a soft grade pencil from 2B up to 4B

LEARNING:

1. Teacher demonstration
2. Flat two-dimensional
3. The effect of light on form
4. Art terminology — cast shadow
5. Teacher demonstration

MOTIVATION: Simple small objects, paper and pencils are distributed to the pupils. They are now asked to draw the outline of the object lightly, and then asked to shade in the shape using the pencil sideways (1). When you shaded in the shape, what way did it make the object look (2)? Now place the object in the light and see what happens (3). Is there a shadow? We call this a 'cast shadow' (4). Are all the sides the same tone? No, there is a light side, a darker side and a darker side still. Is the cast shadow as dark as the darkest side? We get the dark and light by the way we apply pressure to the pencil (5). Now see if you can show all this on your paper. When drawings are completed pupils are asked to select a detail and draw it showing the three-dimensional effect on a new sheet of paper. Don't forget to make your drawings big — fill up the paper.

EVALUATION: Work is placed on display. What did you find when you had to fill up the paper with the detail drawing? You had to arrange the tones (the darks and lights) to suit the paper. When you have a cast shadow in your drawing what does it tell us? It indicates to us that there is a strong light. Do artists show this in their pictures often? Did they always show cast shadows in their paintings? Who can remember a picture without a cast shadow? Reproductions of Oriental art may be shown at this stage, or Egyptian, and Byzantine art. These can be compared with Renaissance paintings.

EXPANDING OPPORTUNITIES: Making a tonal study of a chair, desk, or a shoe and relating the dark and light areas to the size of the paper.

LEARNING SITUATION: Drawing a self-portrait, first using the sense of touch and then vision

PROCESS: Drawing

MATERIALS: Cartridge paper, soft pencil, small mirror

LEARNING:

1. Stating the problem
2. Touch
3. Visual
4. The character and likeness of the person
5. One expressive, the other visual approach

MOTIVATION: Arrangement should be made with the pupil before this learning situation to bring a small mirror to school.

Today we are going to draw a self-portrait in pencil (1). The first way we are going to do it is by feeling the form of our own faces with our hands (2). Try feeling the difference in the curves and angles, the movement in and out, the way the nose sticks out and the way the eyes recede, the curves of the mouth and the chin. Paper and pencil is now distributed. When you know the different features of your head try putting them down on the paper.

On completion of the first drawing more paper is distributed and pupils are asked to produce the small mirror. They are asked to look at themselves and make a portrait drawing filling up the paper (3).

EVALUATION: Work is placed on display and pupils are asked to identify one another from the portraits. What should a good portrait tell us (4)? Reproductions of portraits by Van Gogh and Gainsborough or Reynolds (5) could be shown to the class. The difference in the portraits could be discussed.

EXPANDING OPPORTUNITIES: Drawing yourself with a hat on.

LEARNING SITUATION: Expressing a figure

PROCESS: Gesture drawing

MATERIALS: Newsprint, charcoal or soft pencil

LEARNING:

1. Stating the problem
2. We might call it expressing the feeling
3. The whole shape is drawn
4. The street or supermarket for drawing crowds in

MOTIVATION: Today we are going to do a gesture drawing of a figure (1). What is a gesture drawing? It is a drawing showing action and movement. It is drawing the feeling, what the person is doing (2). A gesture drawing has to be done quickly (3). We feel the movement, think of the figure as one whole movement. We won't be able to show any detail such as the fingernails.

A pupil is asked to take up some action pose, bending down, picking something up from the floor, or sweeping action. (This only means two minutes.) Paper and charcoal are distributed and pupils are asked to fill up the page with the gesture drawing. When one pose is finished another pupil takes a different action pose and so on until four drawings are done. More paper is distributed and pupils are asked to create a picture by arranging the different actions.

EVALUATION: Work is put on display. Pupils are encouraged to talk about their arrangement. Reproductions of action drawing by Daumier, Goya or Rembrandt may be discussed. The drawings appear to be scribbles but the important thing is that they are able to capture the movement. The whole figure seems to be completed at once. Do your drawings look like that? How would this type of drawing be useful to us (4)?

EXPANDING OPPORTUNITIES: Drawing a plant in a flower pot, thinking of them as having action and movement.

LEARNING SITUATION: Expressing an idea through a relief print, making use of a previous drawing

PROCESS: Drawing with relief line

MATERIALS: Strawboard for support or the large side of a cornflake box, thick cork, adhesive (PVA), scissors, tempera paint, rollers or brushes for applying adhesive

LEARNING:

1. Stating the problem
2. The printing surface is raised from the background
3. Teacher demonstration
4. Teacher demonstration

MOTIVATION: Today we are going to do a relief print. Who can tell what that is (2)? The raised surface is going to be cord. Select one of the gesture drawings you did the last day, the one you like best, and use it as a model. Strawboard, cord, adhesive and strips of strawboard are distributed. We have to draw the figure this time with the cord. Start at one end and put some adhesive on the cord and press it down on the strawboard. When it sticks apply more adhesive further along sticking and bending until you have the whole figure drawing (3). When all the cord is stuck, apply the paint by rolling it over the cord or dabbing it on with the brush. (If the spaces are too wide between the lines the paint will go onto the background.) (4) Now lay a sheet of newsprint over the block and roll the back of it with a clean roller. Remove the paper and you have the print. You may try a number if you wish.

EVALUATION: Work is placed on display. Let us see who was able to get a clean print. What is the advantage of taking a print? You can repeat the same picture many times. Do artists do this? How do they do it? They draw on stone. What is this called? (Lithography.) When a printer uses a relief block what is it called? (Letterpress.) There are many ways of taking prints. Some reproductions of prints may be discussed.

EXPANDING OPPORTUNITIES: Designing a block using a polystyrine block or a meat tray.

Upper case block letters. Correct formation for cut or drawn letters.

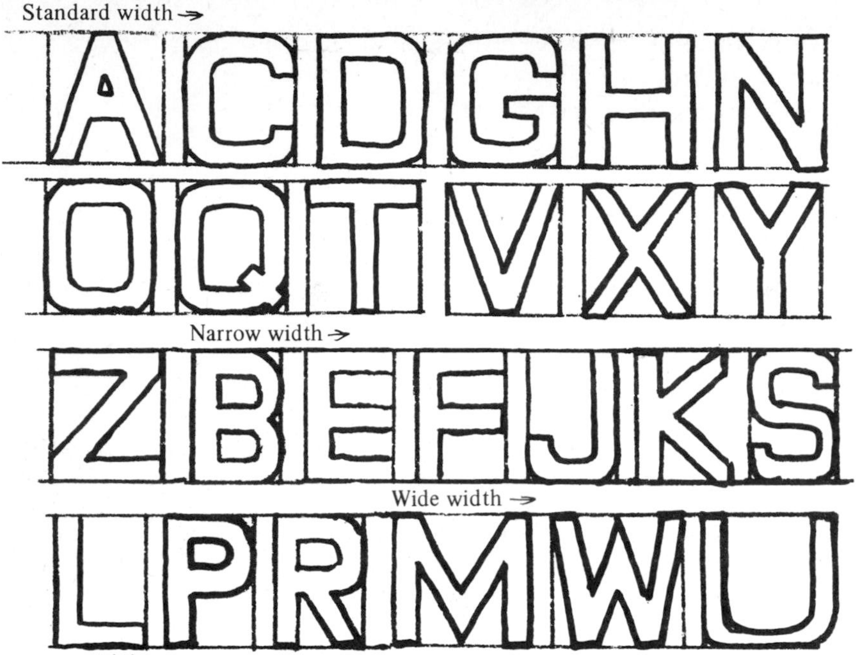

Standard width →

ACDGHN
OQTVXY

Narrow width →

ZBEFIJKS

Wide width →

LPRIMWU

Upper case for poster making

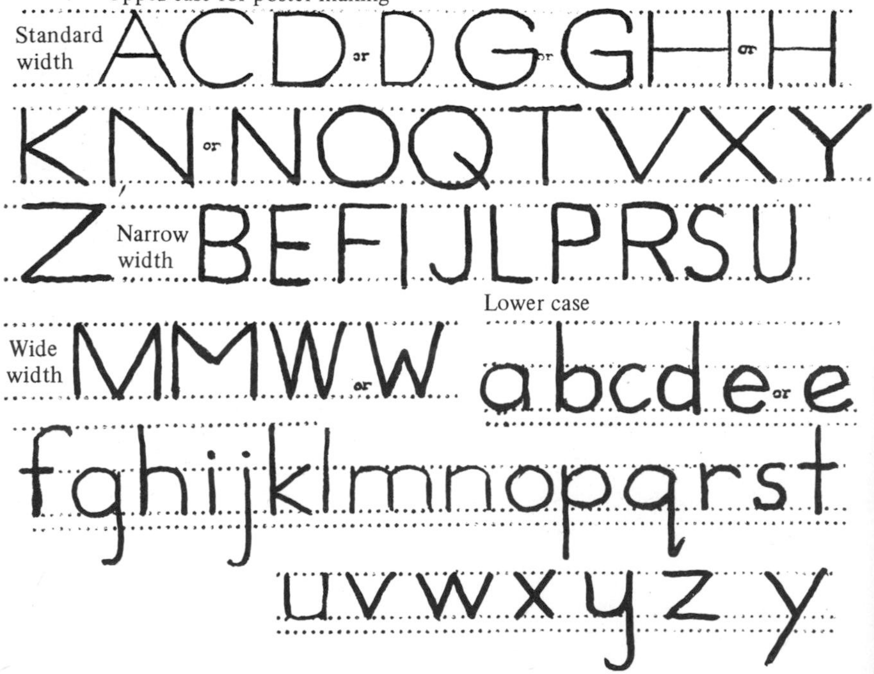

Standard width ACD or D G or G H or H

KN or NOQTVXY

Z Narrow width BEFIJLPRSU

Wide width MMWW or W

Lower case

abcd e or e

fghijklmnopqrst

uvwxyz y

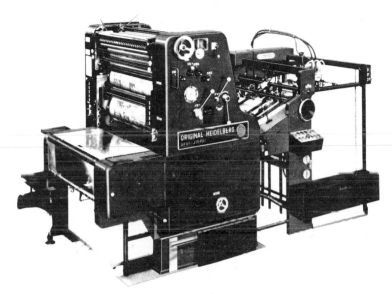

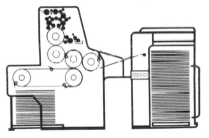

The modern offset printing press prints indirectly from a thin aluminium (or sometimes paper) photosensitive plate, transferring the image to a 'blanket' cylinder (rubber covered) which in turn prints it on the paper.

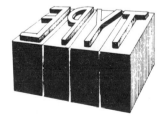

Letterpress (Monotype and Linotype). Type is cast from hot metal (in reverse), inked and pressed directly to the paper. (The impression can often be felt on the paper.)

LEARNING SITUATION: Creating a hand puppet, additive built-up form

PROCESS: Structuring various materials

MATERIALS: Cardboard cylinders (toilet roll centres), different coloured fabrics, tissue paper, adhesive, cold water paste, stapler and staples, knife, scissors, needle, thread, old buttons, scraps of fur, cotton wool

LEARNING:

1. Small figure of a human being, the four principle types are: hand, rod, shadow, string
2. For performing mock drama
3. A puppeteer
4. Stating the problem
5. Teacher demonstration

MOTIVATION: Who would like to tell what a puppet is (1)? What are puppets used for (2)? What is the person who works the puppet called (3)?

Today we will make a hand puppet using a cardboard cylinder for the head; on it we will add a nose and ears made from papier-mâché, cut paper or scraps of fur or cotton wool for hair; the eyes may be made from buttons or painted (4). A section of the cardboard cylinder is cut four centimetres from one end; a vertical cut is made in this section, it is then placed on top of the other section, at an angle, leaving an opening (which forms the mouth) and stapled or glued in position (5). The fabric is used for the clothing which covers the puppeteers hand and arm, forming the body of the puppet. Make the size of the clothing to the size of your hand, measure the distance from the tip of the thumb to the tip of the little finger. To make the costume, fold a single piece of cloth in two, make a cut in the centre of the fold for the neck, then sew up the sides. The costume is then glued in a position half-way up the cylinder.

Everybody must make their own special character and think up a name for him or her. If pupils wish to operate puppets they may crouch down behind a table that has the legs covered with a curtain concealing them from the audience. A more elaborate stage may be constructed from a large cardboard carton.

EVALUATION: Puppets are placed on display and individual pupils are asked to explain their characters. Are puppets a new or an old invention? In ancient times they have been accorded an honourable position. Puppets played the role of teacher of the christian doctrine in the early christian chapels in Italy and France. Who can name some well-known puppets? Each country has their favourite characters: Pulcinella in Italy; Kasperle in Germany; Tchantchés in Belgium; Karagheuz in Turkey and Punch and Judy in England.

LEARNING SITUATION: Expressing an idea with shapes and lines and colour

PROCESS: Cardboard stamping

MATERIALS: Cardboard, large and small shapes, tempera paint, large dishes or biscuit tin lids for holding paint

LEARNING:

1. Recalling an experience
2. Stating the problem
3. Teacher demonstration

4. Teacher demonstration
5. Shape contrast or dark/light contrast, colour contrast
6. Unreal

MOTIVATION: Did anybody ever look at the clouds and imagine they saw things in them (1)? Today we will create an imaginary picture from shapes which we will stamp on the paper (2). Cardboard shapes, paints, dishes etc. are distributed. Place a shape flat in the paint then press it flat on the paper making sure that it is to one side of the centre of the paper (3). Now try a different shape, maybe this shape will be smaller than the first one. Try some more different sizes, then see what you have got. When you have made up your mind what it is, make it clearer by adding lines to it. Lines can be stamped by pressing the edge of the cardboard into the paint and pressing it on the paper. Curved lines can also be stamped by bending the cardboard (4). You may use different colours by changing the dishes around.

EVALUATION: Work is placed on display. Did anybody get contrast in their picture? What sort of contrast is it (5)? Did anybody show the ground and the sky? Who remembered to put texture in their picture? Does your picture remind you of a dream? In a dream what way are things (6)? What were the painters who painted dream pictures called? Surrealists. Reproductions of Marc Chagall's or Salvador Dali's work may be shown to the class.

EXPANDING OPPORTUNITIES: Painting a dream.

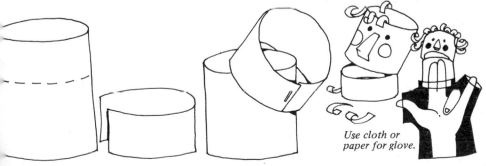

Use cloth or paper for glove.

Measure down 4 cm from top and cut.   *Make vertical cut in smaller section.*   *Staple or glue smaller section at an angle to larger section.*   195

LEARNING SITUATION: Discovering design in everyday objects

PROCESS: Drawing

MATERIALS: Charcoal or felt markers or soft pencils

LEARNING:

1. Industrial designer
2. Height related to figure
3. Stating the problem

4. The design tells about the era
5. New materials require new methods therefore the shapes change

MOTIVATION: Place a school chair on the desk and ask: Who knows what kind of artist designed it (1)? We will all be industrial designers. What is the first thing the designer has to do? He must think where the chair will be used and who will use it. Would an office chair be suitable for everyday school use? Why? Would the height be the same (2)? What material is our chair made from? Paper and drawing instruments are distributed. Pupils are asked to design a chair for a special purpose (3). They must show the side view and the front view.

EVALUATION: Drawings are placed on display. Pupils are questioned as to how they think their chairs will be manufactured. Can we tell from the design something about the time it was made (4)? Why are new shapes being invented (5)? Why has the shape of the telephone receiver changed (5)? Pictures of telephones down through the ages could be shown to the class, or motorcar designs could be examined.

EXPANDING OPPORTUNITIES: Designing a chair from cardboard boxes.

1919   *1928*   *1960*   *1964*

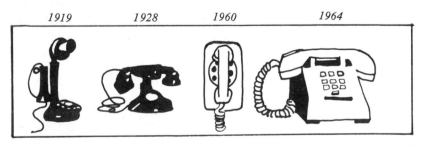

1895   *1900*   *1950*   *1970*

196

LEARNING SITUATION: Creating a relief panel to express pattern and rhythm

PROCESS: Sand casting

MATERIALS: A biscuit tin, fine sand, dental plaster, bowls for mixing, organic forms — bark, shells, stones, twigs etc. — or man made forms — bolts and nuts, scissors, match boxes, wire bent into different shapes etc.

LEARNING:

1. Stating the problem
2. Shapes projecting from the surface
3. On public buildings
4. Teacher demonstration
5. One enhances the other

MOTIVATION: Pupils are asked to bring old biscuit tins and fine sand. Today we are going to design a relief panel (1). Who would like to tell what a relief panel is (2)? Where would you find one (3)? On our panel we will express pattern and rhythm. We all know what pattern is. Show me pattern in the room — the way the desks are arranged. We create pattern for ourselves. We arrange the days. We repeat the way we live. Patterns have always been used. Our breathing has a pattern. In music we have rhythm which is repeated. Look around and get an idea of pattern for your relief panel. Ask pupils to fill the tin with sand leaving an inch and a half at the top. Press down the sand well and damp it with water. Shapes may now be pressed into the surface. Water is placed in the bowl and plaster stirred in until it is a thick pourable consistency. Now it is poured over the sand until the tin is filled to nearly the top (4). It is now allowed to set for some days. When it hardens it may be lifted out by turning the tin upside down, making sure to place paper on the desk to catch the sand.

EVALUATION: Work is put on display. Who thought of the background as part of the pattern? How important is the background to the pattern (5)? Would you say pattern is important to our lives? Patterns have been used down through the ages in art. A photograph of a Gothic style building could be shown to the class. Who would like to guess what influenced the Gothic architects to build in this style?

LEARNING SITUATION: Discovering pictorial composition

PROCESS: Cutting and arranging shapes of colour

MATERIALS: White cartridge paper, grey sugar paper, scissors and paste

LEARNING:

1. Line, shape, colour, form texture
2. Stating the problem
3. Asymmetrical balance
4. Symmetrical balance
5. A large object surrounded by smaller objects

MOTIVATION: When we draw, paint, sculpt, arrange the furniture in the room, dress ourselves, we use the art elements. Who can name the art elements (1)?

Today we are going to create a composition (2). What is composition? It is the way in which we use the art elements placing them together in a whole. You all know what composing in music is or composing a dance or a poem. Paper is now distributed, white cartridge paper and grey sugar paper. Pupils are asked to cut the grey paper into five interesting shapes. We will use these shapes to create the composition. We will use the white paper for support. You have to consider this rectangle because in it we will have to arrange the grey shapes. This will influence your composition. We will call the sheet of paper space. Think how you will start. Many people start by placing the shape in the centre of the space. We won't do that, we will place the shape to one side of the centre. You will want to balance it on the other side with the smaller shapes. You have to arrange the shapes until it feels right to you. Think of it as a scale to which shapes are added on both sides until the scale is balanced. Use your own judgment. When you are satisfied paste the shapes down.

EVALUATION: Put the arrangements on display. Who feels they got a balance? What is the balance called (3)? Is there any other way we can achieve balance? By having equal shapes on both sides. What is that balance called (4)? Reproduction of painting may be examined to see how the shapes are balanced (5).

EXPANDING OPPORTUNITIES: Arranging colours so that the strongest (the one that has the greatest intensity) is balanced by more muted colours.

Composition: balance and rhythm.

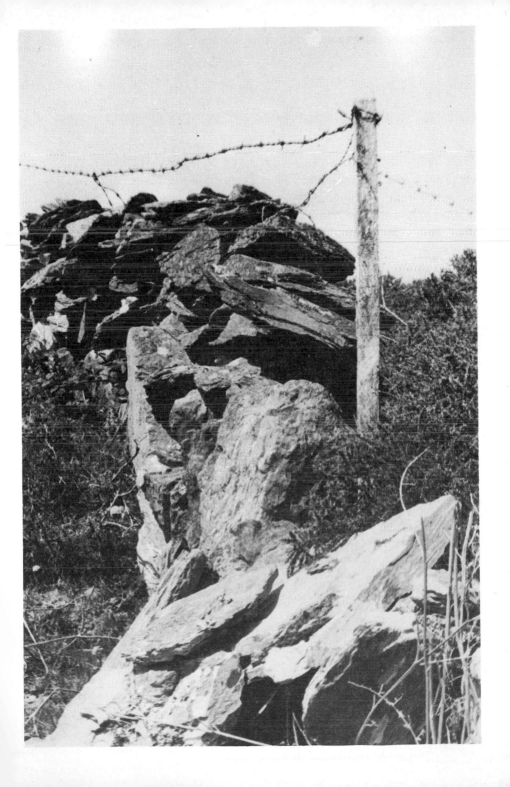

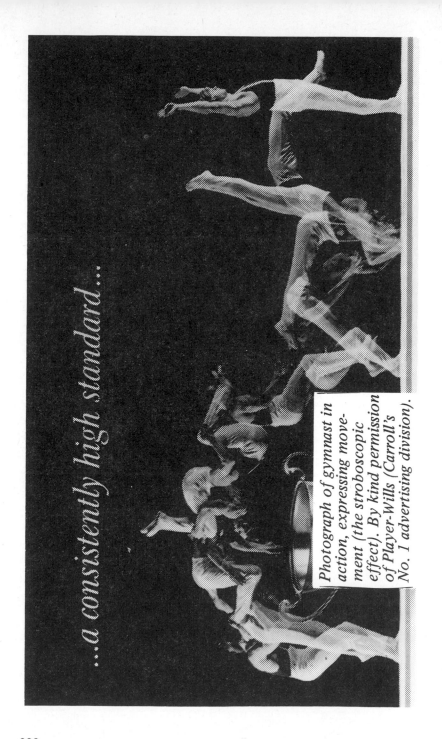

...a consistently high standard...

Photograph of gymnast in action, expressing movement (the stroboscopic effect). By kind permission of Player-Wills (Carroll's No. 1 advertising division).

LEARNING SITUATION: Looking at motion as it occurs in nature. Expressing a kinesthetic experience through a three-dimensional form

PROCESS: Developing form in papier mâché

MATERIALS: Light wire, paste, old newspapers, brushes, bowls for paste

LEARNING:

1. Statement of problem
2. It is the manner in which they are arranged

3. The stroboscopic effect

MOTIVATION: Today we are going to express movement through a papier mache form (1). Who can name things in nature that move and change? (Trees in the wind, clothes on a line, ripples in the water, waves at sea etc.) When you look at movement do you feel it? Who has seen birds gliding? Did you feel the movement when you watched them. Do objects also express movement? Give some examples: the lines of a car, the lines of an aeroplane. Think of some movement, keep it in your mind and express it through papier mache. Bend wire into a form so that it will stand without a support. Wind strips of pasted paper around it until the form is completed.

EVALUATION: Work is placed on display. Let us see now which ones express motion. Does your eye follow lines or shapes that suggest movement throughout the form? How do lines express movement when they don't move themselves (2)? In what way did early man show movement? Reproductions of Lascaux or Altamira paintings may be shown to the class. The reproductions may be examined to see how the animals appear to be moving. Some of Pablo Picasso's paintings express movement (3).

EXPANDING OPPORTUNITIES: Creating a composition that does not show movement.

LEARNING SITUATION: Discovering that spacing in lettering helps the visual effect of words

PROCESS: Arranging examples of type faces or handlettering

MATERIALS: Old magazines, paper for support, scissors and paste

LEARNING:

1. Stating the problem
2. Calligraphy
3. Styles
4. Clear and bold
5. The relationship between the empty space and the letters

MOTIVATION: Ask pupils to bring in old magazines. Today we will look at the way letters are arranged on the printed page (1). Before the invention of printing, lettering had to be done by hand. Do we know what the art of lettering is called (2)? We will select a page in the magazine and turn it upside down, look at it and see which part stands out. Somebody had to design the arrangement of the lettering on the page. We call this the 'layout'. Examine other pages to see what sort of layout they have (3). Look at the white spaces between the printed parts on the page. Support paper, scissors and paste is now distributed. Pupils are asked to pick out certain kinds of lettering. Cut out words or single letters. Look at individual letters as lines and shapes. Look at them as designs and not in terms of their meaning. When you have a number of letters and words arrange them on the white paper so as to form a pattern of heavy and light. Think of the white spaces. They help the letter or words to look well.

EVALUATION: When everybody is satisfied with their arrangements put the work on display. Do any of the arrangements express a meaning beyond the meaning of the word? Do some letters stand out beyond others? Why (4)? Are some weak? Are others enjoyable in themselves? What type of an artist was responsible for the layout? Reproductions of illuminated letters or pages from the Book of Kells could be shown to the class. Their decorative effect could be discussed (5).

EXPANDING OPPORTUNITIES: Creating a letter style appropriate to the message.

SMART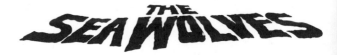

UNIQUE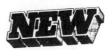

This is normal letter spacing: STOP

This is condensed letter spacing: STOP

This is widely spaced: STOP

This is more widely spaced: STOP

CONDENSED   NORMAL   SPACED OUT

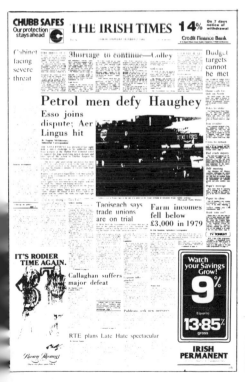

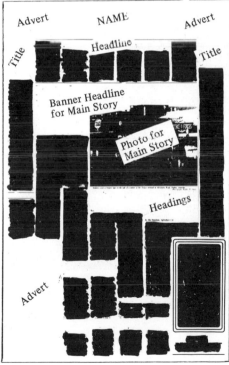

ooking at design in a daily newspaper. Analyse the space relationships by blackening over all the text. *he above example has a layout based on an eight column vertical grid. Advertisements at top and *ottom (left and right) give balance. Note strengths of various headline letters; use of single and *ouble-column line widths. Note the off-centre position of photograph.

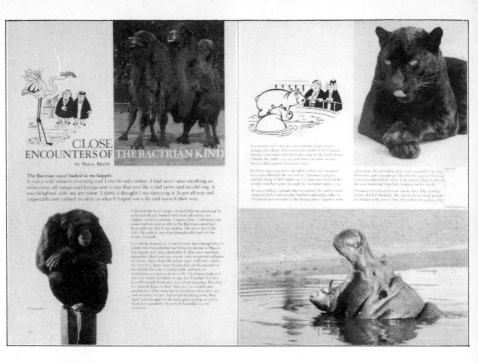

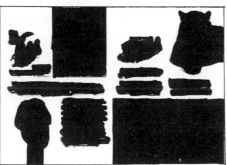

Generous use of white space in a double page spread of a magazine. Pupils could cut up magazines and rearrange the different elements to create their own layout designs. Compare with newspaper example on page 203.

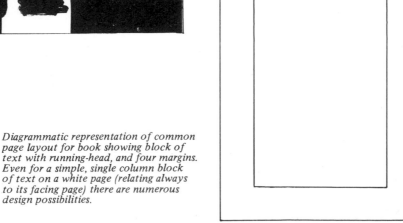

Diagrammatic representation of common page layout for book showing block of text with running-head, and four margins. Even for a simple, single column block of text on a white page (relating always to its facing page) there are numerous design possibilities.

LEARNING SITUATION: Designing a stage set or a diorama

PROCESS: Arranging shapes in actual space

MATERIALS: Any suitable boxes such as a shoe box, old newspapers, construction card, cellophane, twigs, scissors, tempera paint, brushes and containers for water, mixing dishes, paste, wire

LEARNING:

1. Stating the problem
2. By painting shapes that show distance on the back of the box
3. The back of the box
4. Papier maché
5. Twigs
6. A stage set

MOTIVATION: Today we are going to make a diorama (1). A diorama is an arrangement of shapes or forms in a box that has the front open, the back of it closed. The space is only from the front to the back of the box. How could you extend the space (2)? We will think of a fantasy scene. It can be set against a background (3). We can place figures (4) in the scene or trees (5). Do not forget to think of the title.

EVALUATION: The dioramas are placed on display. Individual students are asked to talk about their fantasy scenes. What does the diorama remind you of (6)? Let us see who thought of grouping. Are the figures grouped? Are the figures grouped on the stage? Do you think they use grouping in films? What are these groupings like?

EXPANDING OPPORTUNITIES: Designing a panorama which is set up with the view open on all sides.

LEARNING SITUATION: Creating an arrangement of textured shapes to express depth

PROCESS: Collecting printing textures and arranging them to express an idea

MATERIALS: Old magazines, scissors, paste, paste brushes, containers for paste, cartridge paper for support

LEARNING:

1. Stating the problem
2. Rough and smooth etc.

3. Few houses, soft curving shapes in the country scene
4. Multiples of verticals, horizontals and diagonals, rectangles for windows etc. in the city scene

MOTIVATION: The last day we used actual space to express an idea. Today we are going to use textures to express space (1). Pupils are asked to search for printed textures in the magazine pages. When they think they have collected enough, scissors, paper for support and paste are distributed. Think of some scene, the way you did the last time. Maybe it is a landscape, a village or a city scene. You must try and show distance in your scene.

EVALUATION: Work is placed on display. Do we have contrasts in these compositions? What are the contrasts (2)? Are there any differences between the textures you find in a country scene and a city scene (3)? What is the main difference (4)?

EXPANDING OPPORTUNITIES: Designing a texture for a print design.

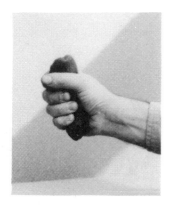 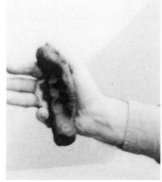 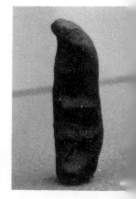

See Fifth Class No. 18.

LEARNING SITUATION: Designing a handle for a tool — discovering the relationship of the handle to the hand

PROCESS: Modelling

MATERIALS: Plasticine, old tools and pots without handles

MOTIVATION: There are many reasons why things look as they do. Sometimes we can tell what a thing is from its shape. The concept of shape may be discussed. A volume appears as a shape when viewed from any one side.

Today we will think about hand-held objects. Who can tell about a hand-held object? Objects with missing handles are put on display, e.g. old pots, screw drivers, hammers, old saws. Pupils are asked to design handles for the old tools.

Plasticine is now distributed. Ask the pupils about the size of the handle. Would the handle of the pot be the same size as the handle for the screw driver? Is the texture important? Should we have a place to fit the thumb and the fingers, so as to give a grip. Pupils may grip the plasticine so as to take an impression of their grip. Would there be a difference in a handle that you lift and a handle you twist or push? Would we design this handle for one person or many? That means we must think of the varying hand sizes. When you have finished, make a drawing of the moulded form, full size. See now if you would have to alter it so as to fit the different sized hands. When pupils have completed the handles they may be placed on display.

EVALUATION: Let us see if we can guess which handles are for pushing, twisting and lifting. Would we be able to figure out their uses from their shapes? How would we decorate these shapes? If we put leaves on them do you think that would be a suitable decoration? Why? (It might disguise its function.) So we cannot let the decoration of the object disguise its function, it must enhance it.

EXPANDING OPPORTUNITIES: Discovering how the shape of a claw hammer might evolve.

LEARNING SITUATION: Expressing emotions and feelings through colour – the emotional effect of colour

PROCESS: Tearing, arranging colour shapes

MATERIALS: Tissue, white cartridge paper for a support and paste

LEARNING:

1. Stating the problem   2. Procedure

MOTIVATION: We are going to look at colours and discover meaning that might be present in them (1). Colours have a variety of meanings for each of us. Large squares of different colours are displayed and pupils are individually asked their reactions to them. Pupils are questioned about their responses. How does it make you feel? Why does blue make you sad? Think how you arrived at that meaning. When a satisfactory number of definitions have been given, tissue and cartridge are distributed. Pupils must now select, tear and arrange the colour shapes to express a mood. When they are satisfied with their arrangement they may paste down the shapes.

EVALUATION: Arrangements are placed on display. Pupils are asked to identify the different moods and answers are verified by the owners of the arrangements. Some reproductions of German expressionists could be shown to the class and they could be analysed for their colour content.

EXPANDING OPPORTUNITIES: Expressing temperature through colour, e.g. hot, cold, medium.

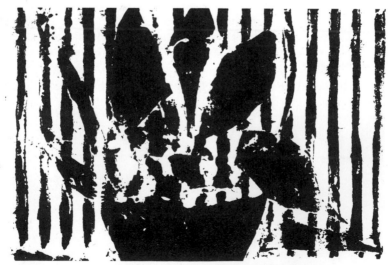

Collography – print from corrugated cardboard. Fifth Class No. 20.

LEARNING SITUATION: Discovering dark on light and light on dark (counterchange) printing from cardboard

PROCESS: Collography

MATERIALS: Cardboard with corrugated centre, lino cutting tools (the knife blades and straight handles), waterbased printing ink, rubber brayers, plate glass or rectangles of 'wearite' or suitable table tops for rolling out ink, newsprint, old sheets of newspaper for protection

LEARNING:

1. This involves cutting shapes out of cardboard, inking the entire surface and printing

2. Teacher demonstration

3. Paper is placed down on the inked surface and the back surface is rolled with a clean brayer, then paper is slowly removed making sure there is a good sharp impression taken

MOTIVATION: Today we are going to try a type of printmaking that you have not done before. It is called collography (1). The cardboard we will use has a flat top surface, a corrugated centre surface and a flat bottom surface. In some areas we will cut right down to the bottom surface, in another area we might just cut away the top surface exposing the corrugated surface and in others we might leave areas of the top surface (2). The picture we are going to print will have light on dark and dark on light.

We call this counterchange. Who can remember seeing pictures with counterchange in them? Some prints of the German expressionists may be shown to the class and discussed. Materials are now distributed. Cardboard, cutters and pencils. Now draw your ideas on the cardboard, don't forget to think of the shapes that are dark. Some of these shapes may be on black horizontal lines or they may be white shapes on dark areas. When blocks are ready, centres are made ready for inking and printing the block (3).

EVALUATION: Prints are placed on display. The quality of the prints is first discussed. Who can identify what is expressed in this picture? Are there any with a sense of movement? What else have we got besides movement? Who thought of large shapes and small shapes? Did anyone make good use of the horizontal lines? Is counterchange to be found in nature? (The dark tree branches going up into the light sky or the trunk of the tree light against the dark foliage.)

EXPANDING OPPORTUNITIES: Pupils may investigate ways of making two colour prints.

LEARNING SITUATION: Creating forms which express a balance of line against plane, lines which define shape

PROCESS: Stabile construction

MATERIALS: Drinking straws, scissors, adhesive, rectangles of cardboard for support

LEARNING:

1. Stating the problem
2. Teacher demonstration
3. Line and shape
4. Space
5. Enclose the space or give direction — advancing, receding — balance

MOTIVATION: Today we are going to construct a stabile (1). We all know what a mobile is. It is a sculpture form that has moving shapes and usually hangs from the ceiling. A stabile remains stable, it does not move. It is made of one material, e.g. string, wire, cardboard, metal. Our stabiles will be made from drinking straws. The stabile will be built on a support. The materials are now distributed. Two short cuts are made opposite each other at the end of a straw, it is folded back and adhesive is applied to both flaps. Press the flaps down on the cardboard support until they adhere (2). A number of straws are set on the cardboard support in this manner. Cut the end of a straw (approx. 1 cm in length) so that it divides in half, press the two flaps, add adhesive and press onto cardboard stand. A number of straws are set up in this manner in order to build a support for the stabile. Other straws can be placed horizontally and vertically to develop the form, on these supports.

EVALUATION: Works are placed on display. Who can tell what the important elements in these stabiles are (3)? What else can we find (4)? How are the lines related to the space (5)? What else would we expect to find (5)? In what way does Henry Moore's sculpture resemble this type of sculpture? They both include the surrounding space. Henry Moore leaves the open holes and we have open spaces.

EXPANDING OPPORTUNITIES: Creating forms with folded strips of construction card or cartridge paper so as to express height and width.

LEARNING SITUATION: Relating the human figure to shape

PROCESS: Cutting paper shapes

MATERIALS: Black paper, white cartridge paper, scissors, adhesive, cardboard strips for spreading adhesive

LEARNING:

1. Shape   3. Counterchange
2. Procedure

MOTIVATION: Ask a pupil to stand in front of a brightly lit window. Request the class to half close their eyes and look at the figure. Ask them what element do they see.

A sheet of black paper and of white cartridge paper and a pair of scissors are distributed to each pupil. Pupils are asked to cut through the two sheets of paper. They are now asked to repeat cutting the shapes from the remaining part of the two sheets. Another black and a white sheet are distributed to each pupil and they are asked to arrange the black and white shapes so as to have a black on a white and a white on a black (counterchange). When pupils are satisfied with their arrangements, adhesive is distributed and they paste down the shapes.

EVALUATION: Work is placed on display. What do we call this arrangement (3)? Man has been using the human figure as a subject down through the ages. Show the class photographs of figures from magazines. What features do we see most often? Are they stout or slim figures? Has man seen the figures the same through the ages? Show the class reproductions of Egyptian and Greek classical figures and reproductions of Henry Moore's sculpture. The Greeks decided on an ideal for the human figure. They measured the foot 6½ to 9 times into the figure. It was not what they saw but what they determined it should be. Would you see any resemblance between Greek sculpture and Henry Moore's sculpture? Henry Moore designed his figures for outdoor setting and so did the Greeks. The Greek figures are solid. Henry Moore has holes in his so as to bring in the space around them. What did Picasso show?

EXPANDING OPPORTUNITIES: Drawing figures to represent a new ideal (Fashion drawing).

Renaissance artists used a unit of measurement which was the foot or the head of the figure. They varied between six and nine multiples of "feet". Leonardo da Vinci used to make his figures the sum of nine "heads".

LEARNING SITUATION: Creating a symbol by working with cut and torn paper

PROCESS: Working with torn paper

MATERIALS: An assortment of coloured papers or colour printed pages from magazines, paste, cartridge paper for support, scissors, cardboard strips for spreading paste

LEARNING:

1. Traffic signs etc.
2. It is a means of quick communication
3. Wash your hands — Waste paper — Keep yard tidy — Quiet please

MOTIVATION: I am sure you all know what a symbol is. Where do we normally find symbols (1)? Why do we use symbols (2)? Has anybody got any suggestions for symbols that we may place in the school corridor or the cloakroom or school yard or near a school activity (3)? When pupils have considered their ideas, materials are distributed. Pupils are asked to create symbols and are asked to try and make the symbol fill the format.

EVALUATION: Symbols are placed on display. Pupils are asked to read what each individual has communicated. The class is encouraged to discuss the different merits of the symbols. Is it the shape or the colour that helps us to read the symbol? Why are we using symbols more and more? (International communication.)

EXPANDING OPPORTUNITIES: Creating trade symbols — building firm, furniture removal, saw mills.

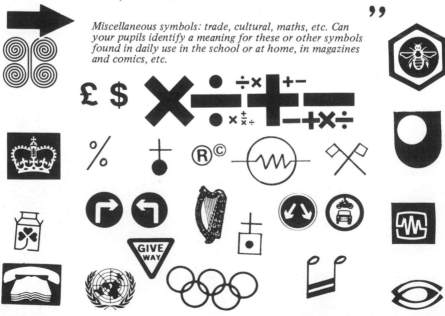

Miscellaneous symbols: trade, cultural, maths, etc. Can your pupils identify a meaning for these or other symbols found in daily use in the school or at home, in magazines and comics, etc.

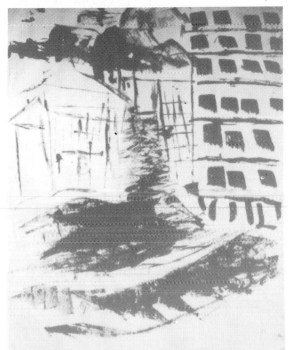

Street scene.

Drawing with

cardboard tool.

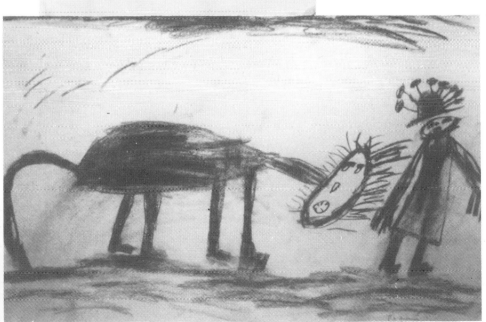

'Attacked by fierce lion.' Charcoal drawing expressing a feeling.

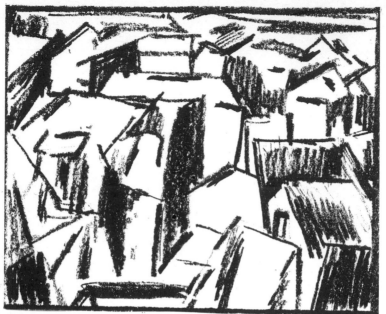

Houses expressed in a cubist way (after Picasso).

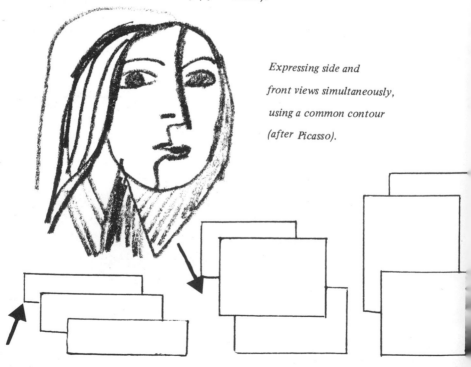

Expressing side and front views simultaneously, using a common contour (after Picasso).

Movement engendered by overlapping planes. Refer also Sixth Class No. 6.

LEARNING SITUATION: Drawing a figure showing more than one side at a time

PROCESS: Drawing

MATERIALS: Cartridge paper or newsprint, charcoal or soft pencils or crayons

LEARNING:

1. It was made two-dimensionally   3. Stating the problem
2. Teacher demonstration

MOTIVATION: A pupil is invited to sit before the class. How could we draw a figure showing different sides at the same time? A box is opened out so that all the sides are shown flat by way of demonstration (1). What did we do with the box when we opened it out (2)? We will change the figure from three-dimensional to two-dimensional. We will draw all sides the same distance from the viewer and arrange all the views so that they fill the paper and make a whole or unify them (3).

EVALUATION: Work is placed on display. Reproductions of cubistic work of Braque or Picasso are shown to the class. Pupils are asked if there are any similarities between their work and the reproductions. Who knows what this style of painting is called? It is called 'cubism'. Pupils are asked to note that there is no illusion of depth in the pictures. The objects are twisted around showing all the views stacked up on top of each other.

EXPANDING OPPORTUNITIES: Painting figures showing movement. (The Kinesthetic sensation.) A sequence of positions of a moving figure. Giacomo Balla reproductions: Dog on leash'. 'Automobile and noise'.

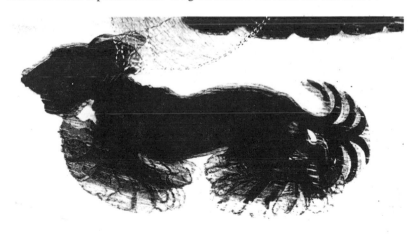

'Dog on leash.' (Giacomo Balla)

Art Growth Characteristics

1. Developing a greater interest in social awareness.
2. Greater detail of features and clothing appear.
3. Work is displaying a greater sense of depth.
4. Tends to approximate the actual hues of objects.
5. Has a better understanding of grouping.
6. Art work tends to be more complete in statement.
7. Obsession with realistic detail.
8. Critical ability often develops in advance of productive capabilities.
9. Is able to describe works of art in relation to their sensory qualities.
10. Can make personal, informed judgements about art.
11. May show a greater interest in design for its own sake.
12. Is becoming increasingly aware of adult standards of representation in art.

Behavioural Objectives (intended outcomes for the pupil)

Pupils will be able to:
Understand the linear treatment of a subject
Understand the relationship of the part to the whole
Understand depth on a two-dimensional surface
Understand space relationships
Understand how to express volume
Express in a three-dimensional form
Understand pointillism
Understand expressionism
Understand the visual communication of a word
Understand the expressive meaning in forms
Understand functions of the artist

Pupils will be able to manipulate media and tools:
Drawing with different tools
Cutting and arranging paper shapes
Painting in tempera paint
Cardboard construction
Lino cutting
crayon etching (Sgraffito)
Papier maché
Modelling in clay

SIXTH CLASS

Learning Situations

1. To develop an understanding of linear treatment of a subject by looking for, identifying, comparing and contrasting lines and their relationship.
2. Looking for repetition in nature that is constant.
3. Discovering that everybody has unique physical characteristics and expressing these through line and colour.
4. Discovering the relationship of the part to the whole.
5. Exploring the relationship of space and shape.
6. Discovering that two-dimensional space may be treated to show depth.
7. Expressing irregular forms through contour line drawing.
8. Exploring how flat planes work with internal space relationships.
9. Creating a two-dimensional shape from a given number of identical shapes.
10. Discovering that shadows are created from what light sources there are.
11. Discovering that shadows on an object help to explain the volume.
12. Expressing a form through line and then expressing a close-up of one part of it.
13. Expressing an idea through a relief print — a lino-cut.
14. Expressing an idea through line (sgraffito).
15. Expressing movement through a three-dimensional form.
16. Completing an incomplete picture.
17. Discovering that reflections become shapes.
18. Expressing ideas or feelings that are opposite in character.
19. Making a feeling portrait. Imagining you are under red or blue or green light (collage).
20. Designing letter forms to correspond to the idea of words.
21. Designing a poster.
22. Making models (enlarged) of buds, blooms, seedheads.
23. Modelling a form which expresses an idea of taste.
24. Discovering some of the motives behind visual works of art and the needs they fulfil.

LEARNING SITUATION: To develop an understanding of linear treatment of a subject, by looking for, identifying, comparing and contrasting lines and their relationships

PROCESS: Drawing

MATERIALS: Newsprint 38 x 25cm, tempera colour, any flexible material, cardboard strip, felt markers, sponge strips or charcoal, dishes, jars for water, cleaning-up material.

LEARNING:

1. Kinetic recall   3. Process
2. Stating the problem

MOTIVATION: If you suddenly fell down the stairs or if you went swirling up in the air, what kind of line would you use to describe it? (Discuss various imaginary (1) dramatic situations and let each pupil choose their own). Show on your paper the kind of line that would tell how you felt (2). Would it be thin, delicate or strong; would it be twisting or swaying from side to side? Would it be spiraling? (What is spiraling? What direction would it take? Vertical, horizontal?) Maybe you would like to cut your paper into a thin panel or a wide panel. Think what best would suit your 'feelings'. If you have background spaces in between the lines you may fill them in with related lines, that is, lines that move in a similar way to the main lines. Would we make these lines as strong as the main lines? No. If you are using charcoal you must fix it in case it rubs. You may put a very light colour wash over the whole paper (3).

EVALUATION: Who made their 'feeling' line strong? Is there a movement covering the entire surface? What about the in-between areas — did you make the lines interesting in size and colour? What colour 'wash' did you brush on the whole design and why? Were lines ever used like this long ago to express movement? Examples may be shown of Newgrange, high cross decorations, Maori decoration etc.

EXPANDING OPPORTUNITIES: Similar lines and shapes and colours may be used to convey various moods.

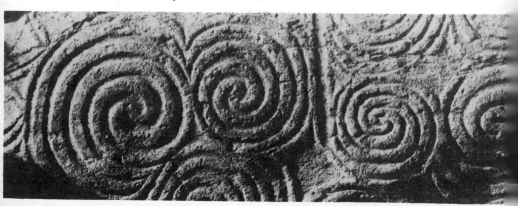

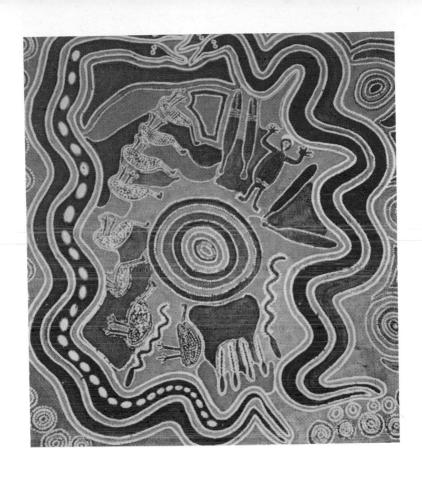

Opposite: Line. From entrance stone to Newgrange tumulus Co. Meath, Ireland c.3000 B.C.

Above: Line shape and colour. Australian aboriginal art. Painted on board.

LEARNING SITUATION: Looking for repetition in nature that is constant

PROCESS: Tearing and arranging random shapes and pasting them down. Also painting with tempera paint

MATERIALS: Paper supports, paints

LEARNING: Perceiving

1. In uniformity with each other – constancy
2. Proximity and distance Things that tend to group together
3. Spaces, shapes, sizes, togetherness, distance, regularity in irregularity. Constancy
4. Regularity and conformity
5. Seek examples of this, e.g. night/day, Winter/Summer. Shapes in buildings, shapes of hands, leaves, stones. Conformity with individuality
6. Confine choice of colour to grey and white

MOTIVATION: Distibute a sheet of paper as a support (size A3). Distribute a second sheet of paper of a different colour (size A5). Ask the pupils to tear the smallest sheet of paper into small pieces (maximum of seven). Drop these pieces from a height (at chin level) by spinning the fingers and allowing the pieces to fall naturally onto the large support (1). Ask the children to observe the resultant arrangement. Did some pieces tend to fall together and some further away? Are some of these shapes close to one another? Are some away from each other (2)? What does not change, and what does change in your arrangement? Is there something that repeats all the time (3)?

Distribute a selection of small branches from a shrub with many interesting irregular features and look for the order in which the shapes repeat, with emphasis on proximity, distance and constancy (4).

Ask the children to paint these discovered shapes with the brush on the format. The torn shapes could also be used in the arrangement by pasteing them down (5 & 6).

EVALUATION: Do we find that things repeat in a regular way, rather than in an irregular way?

EXPANDING OPPORTUNITIES: To assemble a three-dimensional form with a variety of materials and decorate it with a suitable colour to obtain uniformity.

LEARNING SITUATION: Discovering that everybody has unique physical characteristics, and expressing this through line and colour

PROCESS: Brush painting (line) with tempera colour (limit amount of colour)

MATERIALS: Paper, tempera paints, brushes, sticks, feathers, combs, etc.

LEARNING: Perceiving

1. Looking for and identifying visual characteristics

2. Stating the problem

MOTIVATION *(Visual and Verbal)*: We shall try to look closely at all the different types of lines within the figure. Direct students to look at their neighbours. Ask them to state what different details they see within the figure (1), for example the lines that make up the hair, eyebrows, eyelashes and details of clothing such as linear pattern. The linear texture of fabrics, plaids, etc. Do these details move in a certain way? Do they twist, bend, zig-zag, wind, go around? For example, shoe laces, hair bands, collars, buttons, fingers.

Select from your neighbour (figure) one detail that contains many interesting and exciting possibilities for discovery. Draw them. Try different tools and discover whether the marks they make are the most suitable for your detail (2). When you have completed the first detail, maybe you would like to do some more to the page.

EVALUATION: Ask the pupils to examine the lines they have made and discern lines that flow, continue, radiate, form clusters of dots, or broken lines. Which tool did you find the most expressive?

EXPANDING OPPORTUNITIES: Selecting tools on the basis of their suitability to express an idea.

LEARNING SITUATION: Discovering the relationship of the part to the whole

PROCESS: Painting with tempera paint. Using grey, white on black

MATERIALS: Two paper supports, tempera paints, brushes, mixing dishes

LEARNING: Perceiving

1. Silhouette
2. Parts of the whole

3. Transforming the parts and the shape into a new whole
4. Unity

MOTIVATION: How would you like to select a natural form or a shape in the room? Instruct the pupils to look at the object with half closed eyes and ask them to focus on the solid shape against the light (1). Look at the shape from different angles and select the solid shape you find most interesting and make a large drawing of it on your sheet of paper.

Look again at your object, but this time focus on the inner detail and shapes within the solid shape (2) and make drawings of these parts.

Select the whole and the parts you like best and put them together on your sheet of paper to form another whole. Keep adding parts until you make a new whole (3). Some parts may be foreground parts and other parts may be background ones. Don't forget to make some parts dark and some parts light.

EVALUATION: Compare the parts to the wholes. In what way do they repeat each other? Size, texture, pattern, shape. In what way do they differ? Do all the new parts you have added make a whole (4)? Do we find that some parts are dominant and some parts subordinate?

EXPANDING OPPORTUNITIES: Make a three-dimensional cardboard construction having dominant parts and subordinate parts — figure — for construction with boxes.

LEARNING SITUATION: Exploring the relationship of space and shape

PROCESS: Cutting paper, arranging and pasting

MATERIALS: Three sheets of both white and grey sugar paper, scissors, paste, cardboard strips for spreading paste, pages from magazines folded for holding paste

LEARNING:

1. Procedure
2. Stating the problem
3. Space size
4. The size of the site
5. Shape in poster design, type on the page of a book, book cover design

MOTIVATION: A sheet of white and grey sugar paper is distributed to each pupil (1). Pupils are asked to concentrate on the sheet of white paper. We will call this sheet of white paper a space, as you know it has four edges. In this space we are going to arrange shapes to make it appear small (2). Scissors and paste are now distributed. Pupils are asked to cut shapes out of the sheet of grey paper and arrange them in the space making it appear small. When they are satisfied that the space appears small they may paste down the shapes. Now the second two sheets are distributed and pupils are asked to cut and arrange grey shapes in it, to make it appear big, again pasting down the shapes when they feel the space is big. What happened to the shapes in the first space? They do not appear to advantage. They are too big, they have eaten up all the space. In the second one what happened? The shapes are lost in the space. The last two sheets are now distributed. Pupils are asked to cut grey shapes and organise them in the space, to allow the eye to move freely through the space from one shape to the other. Paste down the shapes when you are ready.

EVALUATION: Work is placed on display. When we were fitting the shapes into the spaces were we designing? When we are designing we often have to keep to certain limitations. What limitations had we got today (3)? If you were designing a house what limitations would you have (4)? We call this visual arrangement. Where else do we find problems of visual arrangements? Furniture that 'fits nicely' in the room. What about the windows in buildings? Who can give me more examples (5)?

EXPANDING OPPORTUNITIES: Relating figures to space.

Too much space or poorly organised space.

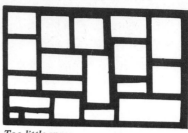

Too little space.

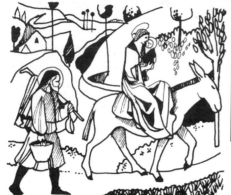

(after Giotto)

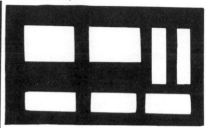

Sufficient space or well organised.

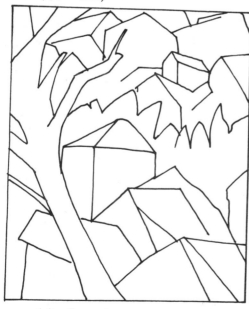

(after Cezanne)

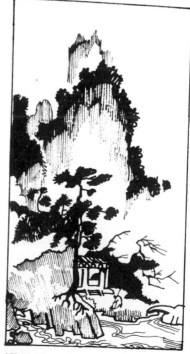

(Chinese)

LEARNING SITUATION: Discovering that two-dimensional space may be treated to show depth

PROCESS: Drawing, painting

MATERIALS: Cartridge paper, black and grey tempera paint, pencil, brushes, mixing dishes, water containers

LEARNING:

1. Foreground, middleground, background
2. Procedure
3. Perspective

4. Now penetrating space
5. The early twentieth century movement with its concern for basic structure combining all sides

MOTIVATION: We know that the sheet of paper is a space surrounded by four edges (sides) and it has a flat surface. But we could also think of it as a space into which we could put ideas and feelings visually. We could see it as a space. We could walk into it (visually).

A pretended space, where the eye wanders from near to further back and still further back (1). We call these spatial levels. We will change the 'feeling' of the space from a feeling of flatness to a feeling of depth. Materials are distributed. First draw lines with pencil so as to make unequal spaces. The lines may touch but never cross each other. When you think you have enough lines drawn to change the feeling, you may fill in some shapes grey, some black and leave others white (2).

EVALUATION: How many were able to change the flat space into a space that shows depth? We could call this 'space treatment'. This has been the concern of man for centuries. Examples of different space-depth treatment may be shown to the class. The Renaissance period with its vanishing points, eye level, receding lines converging at a vanishing point on the horizon lines, which are actually eye level lines, as seen from a fixed view point (3). Oriental art which disregards 'deep' space of the west. Placing forms low on the paper so that they appear to come forward, and high up on the paper so that they appear to recede (2). Cubism, the disregard of the Renaissance-type space with its multiple views and shifting planes. Non-realistic colour or non-adherent to local colour (5).

EXPANDING OPPORTUNITIES: Space depth treatment with textured surfaces.

Opposite: (centre left and bottom left and right).
Space depth treatment. Refer also to lessons: Second Class No. 3 and Fifth Class No. 24.

Space depth treatment. Refer also to lessons: Second Class No. 3 and Fifth Class No. 24.

LEARNING SITUATION: Expressing irregular forms through contour line drawing

PROCESS: Drawing

MATERIALS: Felt pens, crayon (black), charcoal sticks, sheets of cartridge newsprint paper, hats, shoes, bags or vegetables

LEARNING:

1. Stating the problem
2. Procedure
3. Depth. It shows three dimensions and thickness
4. By shading around the contours

MOTIVATION: Who would like to tell what a contour is? Today we are going to make contour drawings (1). We will look and think of the object as if we were touching it with the felt pen. Your eye and the pen will move at the same time along the contour of the object. You will have lines going up and down as well as in and out. You will find the edge does not end on the outline but continues moving inside and then outside. Sometimes the lines meet other lines (edges) or they end.

Paper and tools are distributed to each pupil. One sheet is for drawing on and the second sheet is to stop you from looking at your paper while you are drawing. Hold it in your left or right hand horizontally above your pencil and paper (2). Pupils may place a shoe on the desk or whatever object they choose. They may then commence drawing. Pupils are allowed to continue drawing for a short while and are questioned. What did you find when a line met an edge? You had to stop and start again. Do you find gaps in the drawings at these points. We will commence drawing again but this time everywhere we find lines meeting or changing we will remove the 'hiding paper' and look at the drawing and restart in a new direction until we have the complete form drawn.

EVALUATION: Place work on display. What do we see in these contour line drawings beside contours (4)? Reproductions of line drawings may be shown to the class. A Matisse drawing may be compared with a drawing by Paul Klee of primitive and Renaissance drawings. How was depth shown in Renaissance painting.

EXPANDING OPPORTUNITIES: Drawing contour lines from changing view points of the same object.

LEARNING SITUATION: Exploring how flat planes work with internal space relationships

PROCESS: Cardboard construction

MATERIALS: Strawboard, scissors, rulers, adhesive, protection for work tops

LEARNING:

1. Space
2. The inside space
3. Planes
4. Relating house to landscape
5. Landscaped
6. Integration of building and landscape

MOTIVATION: What would your first consideration be if you were architects and you had to design a house (1)? You would consider the space you had to put the house in (site). What else would you consider (2)? What forms the inside space (3)? The walls. A cardboard box may be used as a demonstration with the lid off. If the site was hilly or flat or rocky or swampy would it make any difference to the angle of the planes.

Today we will design a house for a site that is very rocky and we cannot remove the rocks. Sheets of cardboard are distributed for the site and pupils are asked to cut and join other pieces of cardboard so as to construct a rocky surface on it. This now is the foundation for the house. Pupils are asked to consider the spaces they will require on the inside. More cardboard is now distributed and they are asked to proceed with the work of designing. How to score and fold should be demonstrated. The score should be made on the opposite side to the fold. Pupils should be reminded to leave flaps for the joining of planes. When all houses are complete they may be painted.

EVALUATION: Models are placed on display. Does the house fit in with the terrain or is it obstructive (4)? Has anybody seen a house like that standing out in a dominant position? Does this house remind you of any you have seen? Sometimes we only see a house in the landscape. What does it lack? Surrounding scenery. Do you think the scenery should be designed (5) or should the house be designed to fit the scenery? We talked about unity before. Should we have unity in a house design (6)? What were we concerned with when we were designing? Space, volume, mass. Can these be found in a painting?

EXPANDING OPPORTUNITIES: Designing volumes to fit into spaces; cutting, scoring and folding paper.

LEARNING SITUATION: Creating a two-dimensional shape from a given number of identical shapes

PROCESS: Cutting shapes, arranging and sticking them to a support

MATERIALS: Black or dark toned sugar paper, scissors, cartridge paper, adhesive, cardboard strips for spreading adhesive

LEARNING:

1. Anything taken as one
2. Stating the problem
3. Procedure
4. The large shape reflects the small unit

MOTIVATION: Who would like to explain what a unit is (1)? We are going to construct a two-dimensional shape from a number of units. The units must all fit together with no background showing and form a large shape (2). Black sugar paper is cut into small rectangles 8cm x 5cm approx. Fifteen of these are distributed to each pupil with a pair of scissors and a sheet of cartridge paper. Pupils are asked to cut one black rectangle into a simple shape, repeat it in all the other rectangles to create fifteen units. Pupils are now asked to fit the units together without any space between them to form a large shape. When all shapes are interlocked pupils may paste them down on the support.

EVALUATION: Work is placed on display. Does the large shape give us an idea what the unit was like before it was built up (4)? We can see this in nature. Leaf shapes tell us what the ribs of the leaf are like. We can say shapes reflect the original units from which they grew. Who would like to give me some more examples of this? Flowers (petals); buildings (geometric units); tree shape (the formation of the branches).

EXPANDING OPPORTUNITIES: Creating a form from related shapes. Cut rings from a small branch of a tree and arranging them to create a new form.

LEARNING SITUATION: Discovering that shadows are created from what light sources there are

PROCESS: Pencil work

MATERIALS: Cartridge paper, soft lead pencils

LEARNING:

1. The shadows alter
2. Procedure
3. The artist has the choice and discretion
4. The object
5. Building, sculpture, etc.

MOTIVATION: Stones, paper and pencils are distributed to each pupil. Pupils are asked to place the stone so that the light falls on it and to examine it. When an object is placed in light we see it and also its shadow. The shadows tell us it is three-dimensional. You must decide how many shadows there are and how many you will include in your drawing. See what happens when you move closer to the stone or move it closer to the light or further away from the light. Be sure to observe them carefully, draw them on the paper, matching the dark and light with shading done with the pencil (2). Make sure to fill the space with the shadows.

EVALUATION: Work is placed on display. From these drawings can we know what the real stone looked like (3)? You are the designer, the organiser and planner. What are the shadows made from (4)? We call these the cast shadows. Where else would you find cast shadows? Shadows on objects help to explain the structure (volume) of the form (rounded forms). Photographs could be examined for different lighting effects.

EXPANDING OPPORTUNITIES: The study of shadow forms from photographs, isolating the shadows from the light forms.

LEARNING SITUATION: Discovering that shadows on an object help to explain volume

PROCESS: Pencil work

MATERIALS: Cartridge paper, soft lead pencil

LEARNING:

1. Stating the problem

2. Through colour, producing the illusion of volume in a painting

MOTIVATION: Pupils are asked to bring in a number of small boxes, e.g. cylinders, rectangular prisms. We know what cast shadows are. Arrange these forms so that they cast shadows on each other. Shadows help to explain the volume. We will show the volumes by the use of shading, using the pencil (1). Look at the places where the dark and light areas are. Make a light outline of these areas first, then turn them from flat shapes into volumes by shading with the pencil.

EVALUATION: Work is placed on display. Who was able to get a wide range of dark and light with the pencil? What do we call this range from dark to light? Tones values (weight) . In what other way can we express tone (2)? The word *chiaroscuro* could be introduced (3). Reproductions of Rembrandt and Vermeer could be shown to the class.

EXPANDING OPPORTUNITIES: Drawing a city of the future showing the volumes of the buildings and their cast shadows.

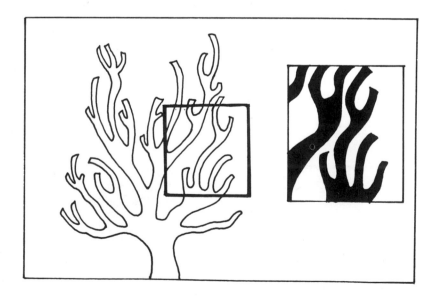

LEARNING SITUATION: Expressing a form through line and then expressing a close-up of one part of it

PROCESS: Drawing with a brush

MATERIALS: Brushes, tempera paint, two sheets of newsprint

LEARNING:

1. Stating the problem
2. Shapes
3. Viewing the objects as shapes, colours and textures
4. Now — objective

MOTIVATION: Pupils are presented with any common object or a plant form and are asked to observe it for its linear content. We are going to examine this object carefully to see how the lines describe it. We will first look at the contour line and then the inner lines and draw these with brush and paint (1).

When pupils are finished the second sheet of paper is distributed. Pupils are asked to focus in on a small part of the drawing (2cm x 2cm approx.). They are now asked to fill this second format with the lines found in the small section. When they have finished, they are asked to fill every alternate space black.

EVALUATION: Work is placed on display. What did the lines we drew produce (2)? Can we guess from the shapes what the original object was like? Does the part explain the whole? Do we find in some paintings that a part gives us a hint and helps us to know what the painting is about? What do we call this type of painting? Abstract. What did the abstract painter do (3)? What do we call this? The objects have been replaced by the elements (line, shape, colour, texture). The painters thought that the viewer would respond better to pure arrangement. Have we got music like this type of painting? The music is arranged so that the sounds made by the instrument create a harmonious tone, they do not depend on nature to make up their symphonies.

EXPANDING OPPORTUNITIES: Rearranging parts of photographs from magazines to create an abstract.

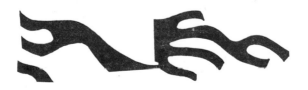

Abstract created by rearranging the shapes discovered in a section of the object (p.230). Each shape combines the character of the square with the character of the object (p.230 inset).

LEARNING SITUATION: Expressing an idea through a relief print — a lino-cut

PROCESS: Lino-cutting

MATERIALS: Linoleum, cutting tools (v-shaped cutters, u-shaped gouges), printers' ink or printing water colours, a rubber roller (brayer), glass on which to spread the ink, newsprint or any suitable paper, cleaning materials

LEARNING:

1. Stating the problem
2. Teacher demonstration
3. Relief printing

MOTIVATION: Today we will make a lino print. We cut into a linoleum block using these special tools. We first will find out how the tools work. Small trial pieces of linoleum are distributed to each pupil and a cutting tool handle and blades. Hold the tool in such a way that it is cutting away from the fingers, in order to avoid accidents (2). The part you cut away will not print. In a good print a fair portion is cut away. Textures can be developed by using various types of cutting tools. The linoleum should always be warm. Paint the lino with white and draw your design with pencil. Think of it as black (the part you leave uncut) and white (the part you cut away). Think about what you are doing, you must take care with the cutting as mistakes cannot be undone. Make the cuts clean and deep to enable you to get clear-cut outlines. When designs are completed, ink is rolled out on a glass surface, spread on a roller and then applied to the block surface. (Tempera paint may be applied with a brush.) Paper is placed down on the block. A clean ink roller is rolled over the surface in order to develop the print. A number of prints may be made.

EVALUATION: Prints are placed on display. Was everybody able to get a good clean print? Have we got a good distribution of the black and white? Have we another name for this type of printing (3)? Some reproductions of German expressionist prints could be shown to the class (Ernst Ludwig Kirchner, Erich Heckel) to show the way shapes were distorted to express emotionalism. Van Gogh and Gauguin were also important in the evolution of expressionism.

EXPANDING OPPORTUNITIES: Rolling colour on an area of paper before making the print.

LEARNING SITUATION: Expressing an idea through line

PROCESS: Sgraffito

MATERIALS: Cartridge paper, crayons, nails or sharp pointed sticks (cocktail sticks)

LEARNING:

1. Expressionism   2. Sgraffito

MOTIVATION: Think of an object, person, place or event that has a special meaning for you, something that you have a feeling for. What painters did we say expressed feeling and emotions (1)? You will express these feelings through Sgraffito.

First cover the white paper with light tone crayon colours, yellow, orange, light red. When you have completed that, cover the whole surface with black tempera colour mixed with soap flakes. Let it dry. Commence scratching into the surface with a sharp pointed stick exposing the underneath colours. Make your feelings fill up the format.

EVALUATION: Work is placed on display. Let us see if we can read the feeling in the pictures. Answers are verified by the owners of the works. What do we call this type of work (2)? (Would it remind you of another way of expressing an idea?) Reproduction of etchings may be shown to the class and the technique could be discussed.

EXPANDING OPPORTUNITIES: Expressing ideas through pen and ink drawing.

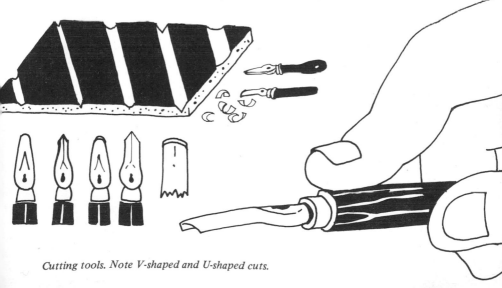

Cutting tools. Note V-shaped and U-shaped cuts.

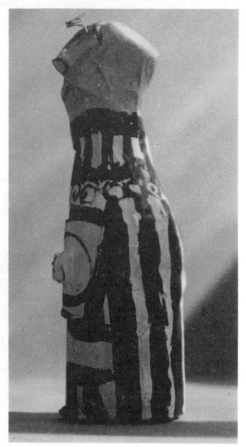
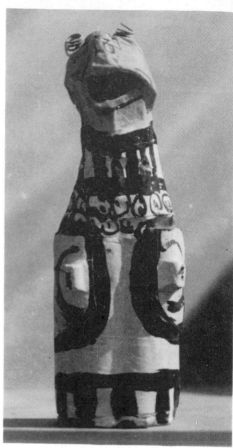

Dip paper strips in water. Wind around bottle until completely covered. Paste further strips and apply to bottle in same manner. Continue with pasted strips until four layers are applied. When dry extract bottle. A head may be added to this papier mâché form. A wire structure on a wooden base can be layered in the same way (see p.236).

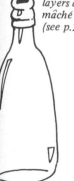
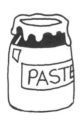
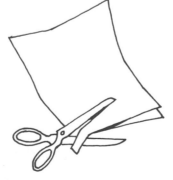
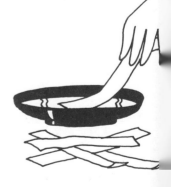

LEARNING SITUATION: Expressing movement through a three-dimensional form

PROCESS: Papier mâché

MATERIALS: Old newspapers cut into strips, thin wire, paste, brushes for pasting, covers for desks

LEARNING:

1. One is visual art and the other performing art
2. Stating the problem
3. We can move around sculpture
4. No longer in existence

MOTIVATION: What is the difference between sculpture and dance (1)? Today we will express movement through something still (2). A pupil is asked to take a pose expressing some action: kicking a football, catching a ball, jumping to catch a ball. Pupils are asked to observe the human shape as it takes up different positions. We will make a figure expressing movement in wire and papier mâché. You will make the framework of the figure in wire. Over this framework we will criss-cross layers of pasted paper until the whole figure is built up. Figures may be painted.

EVALUATION: Work is placed on display. Do all the figures express movement? Do we only see one part of the movement? What is the difference between sculpture and painting? Where is the movement the figure made now (4)? What does the sculpture do that the dance cannot? Why did the Egyptians bury statues with their dead? (Symbols of everlasting life.)

EXPANDING OPPORTUNITIES: Creating movement in animal forms.

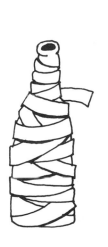
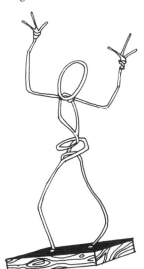

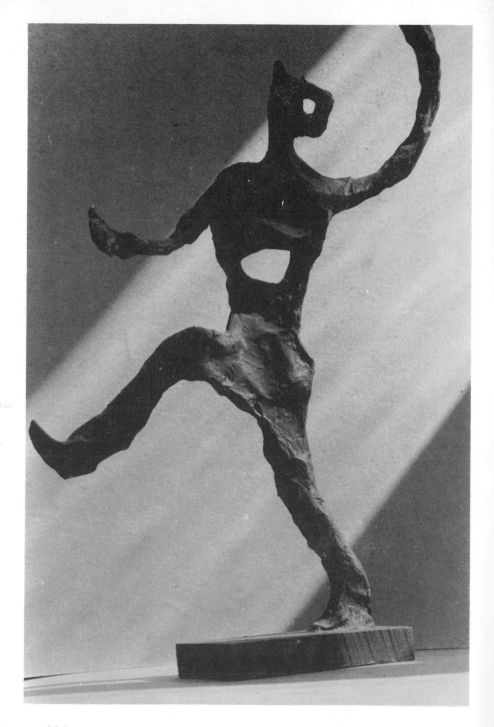

LEARNING SITUATION: Completing an incomplete picture

PROCESS: Painting

MATERIALS: Tempera colour, brushes, mixing dishes, cartridge paper, paste

LEARNING:

1. Stating the problem   3. Surrealists
2. Imagine it

MOTIVATION: Large photographs of forms (figures, faces, hands, cars, machines) are selected from magazines and are cut into two sections. One section of any form is distributed to each pupil along with a sheet of cartridge paper. The pupils are directed to paste the incomplete form in an interesting position on the paper not the centre. How would you complete that form (1)? How do you see the rest of the head? What figure goes with the hands? Think carefully. Study the different lines or shapes or colours. Many possible ways of completing the form will come to you. The form will suggest a background to you, paint it in also.

EVALUATION: Work is placed on display. What had you to do to develop the picture? Is imagining the same as dreaming? In imagining we make it up in our minds. In dreaming it is thoughts when we are asleep. Were there painters who painted dreams? What were they called (3)? Reproductions of Salvador Dali's painting may be shown to the class. They could be discussed as displaying a 'Fantasy'.

EXPANDING OPPORTUNITIES: Painting a recalled dream.

Papier mâché form built up on wire frame set on wooden base.

LEARNING SITUATION: Discovering that reflections become shapes

PROCESS: Pencil shading

MATERIALS: Two sheets of cartridge paper, soft pencil, dark bottles

LEARNING:

1. Stating the problem
2. Extending tonal areas

3. The parts mirror the whole
4. Shop windows, mirrors, lamp reflectors

MOTIVATION: Dark bottles are distributed to each pupil. Today we will look at reflections (1). Who can say what reflections are? They give us back something. What do you call this something? An image. We will examine the bottles and see if they reflect back images. We will call these images shapes. Draw all the shapes you can find in the bottle, shading them in with the pencil. Make the bottle fill your paper. When drawings are completed, pupils are questioned about the reflections. Were some of the shapes in front of others? Did some appear to be on the surface? Pupils are now asked to cut out the shapes and see if they can make a new arrangement on the second sheet of cartridge paper. If there are empty background shapes they may fill them in with further shading (2).

EVALUATION: Work is displayed. Can we still see the bottle in the new arrangement (3)? Would these reflections remind you of any other reflections you have seen (4)? Do reflections in the mirror throw back the image the same size as the object?

EXPANDING OPPORTUNITIES: Creating images to give a fearful feeling. Painting with grey, black and white tones.

Bottle with reflection.

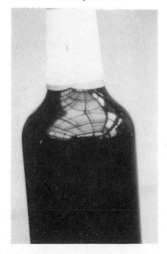

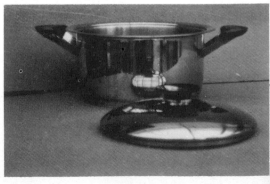

Saucepan with reflection.

Opposite: Reflection in the environment.

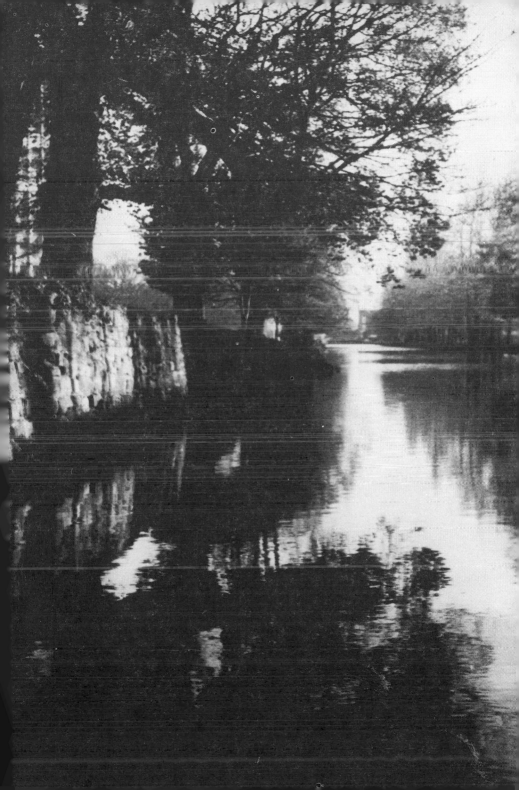

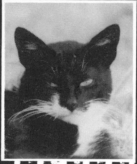

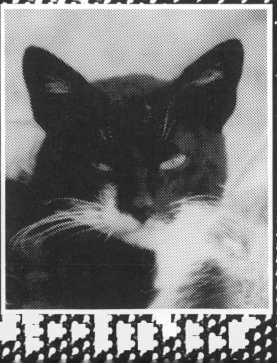

LEARNING SITUATION: Expressing ideas or feelings that are opposite in character

PROCESS: Painting with dots of colour

MATERIALS: Cartridge paper, old wax crayons, candles, jars for holding the candles

LEARNING:

1. Big, small, hot, cold, winter, summer, etc.
2. Teacher demonstration
3. George Seurat (1859–91), Paul Signal (1863–1935)

MOTIVATION: We know that a square is the opposite shape to a circle. Who would like to list some opposites for me (1)? Think of ideas or events that are opposites and relate them, also think of unity and contrast when designing your picture. We will paint this picture with dots of coloured wax. Paper is distributed to each pupil and a candle in a jam jar between four pupils. The candles are lit. The end of the crayon is held in the flame to soften it and then pressed down on the paper forming a wax dot (2). Pupils are asked to complete their pictures in this manner, using the colours best suited to their ideas.

EVALUATION: Work is placed on display. Ideas within the paintings are discussed. How many were able to create unity within their pictures? Do we know any painters who painted by placing dots on the canvas (3)? This style of painting is known as 'pointillism' (to dot or stipple). Reproductions may be shown to the class. Pupils' attention could be directed to the effect achieved by the combination of blue dots and yellow dots when viewed from a distance. It may also be mentioned that in principle this method is like the three-colour printing process. Newspaper photographs could be examined to discover the dots produced by the screen which breaks up the areas of dark and light. It is these dots which recreate the picture.

EXPANDING OPPORTUNITIES: Expressing a form through dots, pen and ink drawing.

Enlargement to show the screen dots which recreate the image.

LEARNING SITUATION: Making a feeling portrait. Imagining you are under red or blue or green light — collage

PROCESS: Painting

MATERIALS: Tempera paint, cartridge paper, brushes, mixing dishes, containers for water, cleaning-up equipment

LEARNING:

1. Realism
2. Expressionism
3. Emotional content of colour
4. Stating the problem
5. A good portrait captures the spirit and the character as well as the likeness

MOTIVATION: We all know that there are two ways of painting: one tries to get close to the 'real' or paint exactly what is seen; the other tries to paint how we 'feel' about things, that is, paint emotionally. Today we will paint a portrait and try to capture the feeling of the person. Try to paint a person you know very well. Think what her/his features are like — the eyes, the nose, the mouth. We are aware how colour can influence our moods, they make us happy, sad, alive, dead, sleepy, angry, nice, cold, hot. Think what colour lightening you will have in your portrait, maybe it will be a blue, red, or yellow bulb. We also know that one colour affects its neighbour.

Equipment is distributed and pupils are asked to make the portrait fill up the space (4).

EVALUATION: Work is placed on display, and discussed. Why did you choose to paint your portrait under that colour light? Can we tell the moods in these different portraits? Do they explain the person's character? Can you describe the person in the portrait? What do you think a good portrait should do (5)? Reproductions of Oskar Kokoschka's and Auguste Renoir's portraits could be shown to the class and the difference between expressionism and impressionism could be discussed.

EXPANDING OPPORTUNITIES: Painting profiles, unusual views using distortion and exaggeration.

LEARNING SITUATION: Designing letter forms to correspond to the idea of words

PROCESS: Lettering

MATERIALS: Cartridge paper, felt pens, rulers, newsprint

LEARNING:

1. Symbol for a sound
2. Stating the problem
3. Letters of a fat character
4. In advertising or packaging
5. It gives a better visual impact
6. The commercial artist

MOTIVATION: We all know what a Roman letter looks like and that it stands for a sound. What is that (1)? When we put these symbols together we have a word. Through the words we 'communicate'.

Today we will try to design letters that communicate the idea of the word (2). For example, the word fat, what way would we have to draw the letters to communicate the idea of fat (3)?

Matterials are now distributed. Think of a word. You may like to try out your letters first on the newsprint. If you wish you may use the ruler to draw light guidelines. When you are satisfied with your letters you may transfer them onto the cartridge paper filling up the sheet with the letters.

EVALUATION: Work is placed on display and the characteristics of the words are discussed. Who has seen this type of communication before (4)? Why do you think this type of lettering is used (5)? It attracts attention. What type of artist is responsible for designing lettering on packages?

EXPANDING OPPORTUNITIES: Communicating the content of a package without lettering.

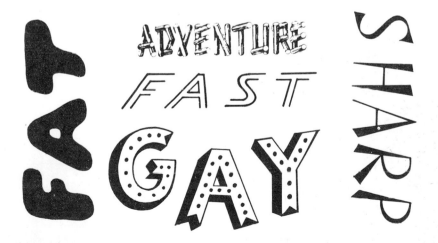

BOOTS

DUBLIN

/ EXHIBITION OF VISUAL.RT /

built

CYCLES

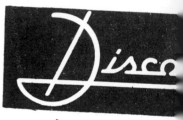

Disco

SETZ

SUPERB SEAFOOD

/ EXILES

IN TOUCH WITH TOMORROW

PERSPECTIVE

LEARNING SITUATION: Designing a poster

PROCESS: Painting and lettering

MATERIALS: Tempera paint, brushes, mixing dishes, water containers, cartridge paper

LEARNING:

1. Stating the problem
2. To catch and hold the attention of the viewer long enough
   to see the message
3. Because posters are placed on
   billboards in from the road

MOTIVATION: We will take on the role of a graphic artist and design a poster (1). What is a poster designed for (2)? What do we find in a poster? Pictures and words communicating something. What would this be? A concert, safety rules, sports events, very often advertising a product with a brand name. Think what you wish to communicate. Materials are distributed. Before you start think what brief you will use and make the words and symbols relate to it. Remember it is very important how you place the letters and illustration in the space.

EVALUATION: Work is placed on display. Which one attracts our attention most? Can we see at a glance what the communication is about? A poster should contain principles of design, i.e. have balance, unity, rhythm and variety. Do our posters contain principles of design? A poster should be large enough to be seen from a distance. Why is that (3)? A poster should be readable from a distance.

EXPANDING OPPORTUNITIES: Design a poster from cut paper.

LEARNING SITUATION: Making models (enlarged) of buds, blooms, seedheads

PROCESS: Modelling

MATERIALS: Clay, old table knives with rounded ends, nylon pallette knives, pieces of stick, old cutlery, empty ball point pens, polythene to protect the desk or small rectangles of hardboard, polythene bags to prevent premature drying of the clay models

LEARNING:

1. Stating the problem
2. To prevent explosions in the kiln if they are to be fired
3. It dried quickly

MOTIVATION: Two buds, two blooms or two seedheads are distributed to each pupil. They are asked to examine them carefully and look for all the shapes present. One may be dismembered carefully and the components laid out in neat bundles. Model these parts but on a much larger scale (1). Reassemble them using the unbroken specimen as a guide. You will have to hollow out most parts and add detail to their surface (2).

EVALUATION: Work is placed on display and discussed. Who was able to get their model to stand? What did we find when working with clay at this scale (3)? When we were reassembling the parts had we construction problems? Why do we make them greater than life size? Do sculptors ever do this?

EXPANDING OPPORTUNITIES: Constructing seedheads from wire.

LEARNING SITUATION: Modelling a form which expresses an idea of taste

PROCESS: Modelling in clay

MATERIALS: Clay, old table knives with rounded ends or plastic pallette knives, pieces of stick, old spoons, empty ball point pens, polythene to protect the desks or small rectangles of hardboard, polythene bags to prevent premature drying of the clay models

LEARNING:

1. Stating the problem

MOTIVATION: Our problem today is to model a form in clay which will convey the idea of a flavour (1). Do musicians only respond to what they hear? Do painters only respond to what they see? We know it is possible to respond through several senses (the ears, nose, tongue) as well as the eyes. Think of one of the following: honey, mustard, peppermint, olives. What flavour has it got? Get the feeling associated with it. Materials are distributed. Model a form which will give us a visual expression of the flavour. Remember the modelled form will not have the outward appearance of the object to which we are responding. (If forms are to be fired the centres must be hollowed out, otherwise they may burst in the kiln.)

EVALUATION: Work is placed on display. The class is asked to identify the different flavours that the forms express. The correctness of the identification is verified with the owner of the form. It may be pointed out that the forms as well as having structure convey ideas. Can modern container jars convey the idea of what they contain? Some containers may be examined for their 'visual expression'.

EXPANDING OPPORTUNITIES: Modelling forms to express the idea of flow.

LEARNING SITUATION: Discovering some of the motives behind visual works of art and the needs they fulfil

PROCESS: Two-dimensional and three-dimensional expression

MATERIALS: Clay, fabrics, paint

LEARNING:

1. Stating the problem   2. Teacher demonstration

MOTIVATION: Today we will think of the reasons why artists create. Could we list some reasons. Explain how pupils' suggestions could possibly fit into the following list:

    Inventing new shapes
    Telling about society
    Recording history
    Expressing religious beliefs
    Decoration
    Expressing inner feelings

Teacher may discuss the various functions of the artist, i.e. industrial design, communications, fashion design, uplifting people from their daily cares. Pupils are asked to adopt one of the above roles and express a concept (1). For example, record a historical event, the landing on the Moon, in one of the media suggested.

EVALUATION: Class work is placed on display. Pupils are asked to discuss the functional content of their individual efforts. Slides or reproductions of the following may be shown to the class (2):

    Egyptian furniture
    Drinking vessels
    Cave paintings
    Communication designs
    Social commentary paintings
    Religious paintings
    Expressionist painting

GLOSSARY OF TERMS

ABSTRACT ART
Art that does not treat subject matter in a representational manner. The forms abstracted from nature are intentionally distorted for expressive purposes.

ANALOGOUS COLOUR
Colours that are grouped next to each other on the colour wheel.

AREA
The space.

ARRANGEMENT
Organising the art elements in a visual unity.

ASSEMBLAGE
Three-dimensional objects placed together in a new context to give special 'visual meaning'.

ASYMMETRY
Visual elements arranged in such a way as to attain an uneven balance.

ART
The adaptation of media by human endeavour as opposed to natural forces to create works that have form or beauty, (aesthetic expression of feeeling as in MUSIC, PAINTING, SCULPTURE, LITERATURE, ARCHITECTURE and DANCE.

BACKGROUND
That part that is furthest back from the picture plane (q.v.).

BALANCE
Obtaining equilibrium among the diverse elements of art in an artistic composition.

BAROQUE
A style of art in the seventeenth and eighteenth centuries, its general characteristics consisted of swirling compositions in painting and curved ornate decoration in architecture.

BAYER
A rubber roller, attached to a handle, mainly used for applying ink.

BYZANTINE
Art from Constantinople Christian art of the Byzantine Empire. The eighth-century manuscript, the Book of Kells, has its links with the eastern shores of the Mediterranean.

CERAMICS
Making earthenware which is fired in a kiln.

CHIAROSCURO
The arrangement of light and shade in a drawing or painting.

CHROMA
The quality of the colour. Chromatically strong, without any sense of grey-ness.

CLASSIC
Formal organisation in terms of Grecian concepts.
COLLAGE
Pasting or sticking discarded materials, i.e. wallpaper, fabric, printed matter on a ground to form a composition. A twentieth-century art form.
COLLOGRAPHY
Printing from cardboard blocks
COMPLEMENTARY COLOURS
Colours that are opposite to one another on the colour wheel (blue—orange).
COMPOSITION
Arranging, structuring the art elements to effect a satisfactory whole.
CONTOUR
Usually a line which indicates the outside edge, the boundary of a mass.
CONTRAST
Opposites, unlike visual elements in a composition.
COUNTERCHANGE
The placement of dark on light and light on dark in a pictorial composition.
CUBISM
An early twentieth-century art movement. The simultaneous presentation of several sides of the same subject so that the painting acquired a flat quality, but retained a plastic element.
DEPTH
The indication of three dimensions, the receding space back from the picture plane.
DESIGNS
The preliminary drawing for a picture, plan, a procedure, the organisation of the art elements in a work of art.
DIORAMA
A diorama recreates in miniature a three-dimensional subject and is usually set in into a three-sided container.
DISTORTION
Departing from the actual form so as to emphasise the expressive qualities in a work of art.
DOMINANCE
Emphasis on certain elements in a composition.
ELEMENTS OF ART
The visual tools, line, shape, colour, texture, tone, space and pattern.
EXPRESSIONISM
The forms of art which convey personal emotions, evidenced by intense fervour in swirling forms and the distortion of shapes and colour.
FAUVES
The wild beasts. A French movement of expressionist painters who used vivid colours and free treatment of form resulting in a decorative effect.

FOREGROUND
That part of the painting which is closest to the viewer, usually the lower area of the composition.

FORESHORTENING
The way forms appear to the viewer from an angle i.e. when a hand is pointed directly at the viewer it appears shorter.

FORM
The totality of the art work. Often used interchangeably with shape. The shape something takes.

FORMAT
The two-dimensional surface on which the artist works, the boundaries are defined.

FRIEZE
A decoration band along the top of a room wall. That part of a Greek temple between the architrave and cornice, often ornamented with figures.

FROTTAGE
An element of texture in the practice of collage French word for 'rubbing', taking a rubbing of grain or pattern on a surface.

FUTURISM
An Italian art movement, it expressed the spirit of the twentieth century in terms of movement, speed and machine forms.

GESTURE
A drawing which attempts to express the essential movement with the figure or form.

GOTHIC
The architectural style from the twelfth century, stain glass windows, thin-walled, pointed-arched buildings.

GRADATION
The gradual change from one colour or tone to the next.

GRAPHIC ART
Art work for printmaking, the technical process of printing, printmaking and photography.

HUE
When the colour is described the hue is named, e.g. a blue-green, a red-orange, warm hues, cold hues.

IMPRESSIONISM
A French art movement of the 19th century. They interpreted the effect of light on objects out of doors and surfaces were broken up by the juxta-position of different hues.

INTENSITY
The brightness or dullness of a colour also called chroma or saturation.

LOCAL COLOUR
The colour which belongs to a particular object e.g. green leaf. The colour you see when the object is removed from all outside optical influences.

MEDIUM
The materials the artist uses to make a work of art e.g. pencil, crayon, paints, wood inks, oil or water for mixing the pigments.

MOBILES
A twentieth-century sculpture which moves about in space. Usually suspended from the ceiling, the shapes creating various spaces and shadows.

MOSAIC
A Roman and Christian art form made from sticking small pieces of stone, ceramic tile, glass to a background.

MURAL
A large painting that is part of the wall, is painted directly on the surface and retains the two-dimensional quality of the wall.

NATURALISM
A style of painting which gives the illusion of objective reality.

NEGATIVE SPACE
The space between and around the positive shapes.

NEUTRAL COLOUR
Colours that do not contain the presence of any hue (black, white, grey).

NON-OBJECTIVE ART
An art form that has no reference to the natural appearance.

PATTERN
A repetition of shapes which is much larger than texture, it can be a decorative design.

PERSPECTIVE
A way of representing objects at varying distance from the eye. A Renaissance development. One of its main principles being that receding parallel lines converge to a point on the horizon.

PICTURE PLANE
An imaginary surface between the viewer and the objects in the painting. Objects are placed back from the picture plane. The two-dimensional surface of the drawing or painting.

PIGMENT
A colour substance which is mixed with a binding liquid to make paint. Usually in powder form.

PLASTIC ELEMENT
Describes the artist's sense of three-dimensional form and his ability to convey it on a flat surface, the in and out movement in the painting.

POINTILLISM
A way of painting with dots of yellow, red and blue as used by the French 19th century painters, it is like in principle the mechanical three-colour process of colour reproduction.

POP ART
An art form which commented pictorially on modern life in the 1960s. Popular imagery of advertisement, photographs of film idols and slogans, as ingredients of paintings and collage.

POSITIVE SPACE
The shape that is surrounded by the space. Areas on the surface.

PRIMARY COLOURS
Red, Yellow, Blue: they do not come from the combination of other colours.

PROPORTION
The size relationship as they exist in nature and human anatomy, comparing parts as to size, quality, variety, scale, purpose, or meaning, e.g. the space of red in relation to a space of green.

REALISM
Representing truthfully form and colour in existing objects without an imitative rendering.

RENAISSANCE
Rebirth; a development in art which began in 14th century Italy and revived interest in the classic productions of the Greek or Greco-Roman world.

RHYTHM
A movement created by the repetition of one or more of the visual elements in a composition.

ROMANESQUE
In pictorial form, the religious painting from the 11th to the 12th centuries.

SCALE
The size of the drawing in relation to the object being drawn.

SECONDARY COLOURS
Colours which contain the mixture of two primary colours

SERIFS
In Roman lettering they are the curved attached terminal points of the letters.

SGRAFFITO
A method of scratching through a dark surface to expose the light colours underneath, giving the effect of a drawing.

SHADOW (CAST)
Shadows cast from solid forms or projections.

SPECTRUM COLOURS
Colours of light obtained by the refraction of a ray of light through a prism, as in the rainbow, violet, indigo, blue, green, yellow, orange and red. Usually considered the colour circle.

STABILE CONSTRUCTIONS
Sculptures that are attached at one point and cannot move, with emphasis placed on balance of line or plane, or space and solid area.

STYLE
The characteristics of an art movement, the way the artist expresses himself during a certain phase of his development.

SURREALISM
A twentieth-century art movement based on the idea of using the sub-conscious as a source for subject matter and expression, the paintings possessed a dreamlike quality.

SYMBOL
A form that stands for something apart from itself.

SYMMETRY
A formal balance of the elements.

TECHNIQUE
The artist's individual manner and mastery of materials and methods.

TEMPERA PAINT
Water-soluble powdered pigments containing a binder which dries opaque.

TESSERA
One of the small pieces of which a mosaic is made.

TEXTURE
One of the elements of art, the surface quality of objects when touched, range from smooth — rough.

TONE
The gradations from light to dark of the hue, sometimes known as value or weight.

TROMPE L'OEIL
A painting that fools the eye and gives the impression of actually being what it represents.

UNITY
A harmonious relationship of the art elements in a work of art.

VANISHING POINT
The point on the eye level to which the receding parallel lines converge. The parallel lines above eye level converge downward while those below eye level converge upwards to meet at the vanishing point, in linear perspective.

VARIETY
One of the principles of visual order.

VOLUME
A form that has dimensions in length, breadth and depth.

BIBLIOGRAPHY

Art in the Elementary School
Marlene M. Linderman. WM. C. Brown Company Publishers, Dubuque, Iowa.
Art Learning Situations for the Elementary Education
Warren A. Anderson, Wadsworth Publishing Company Inc. Belmont, California.
Children and their Art
Charles D. Gaitskell, Al. Hurwitz
Harcourt Brace Jovanovich, Inc. New York.
Creative and Mental Growth of the Child
Vicktor Lowenfeld, Macmillan.
Change in Art Education
Dick Field. Routledge and Kegan Paul.
Art and Visual Perception
Rudolf Arnheim. Faber and Faber London.
Visual Education in the Primary School
John M. Pickering. B.T. Batsford Limited, London.
The Joyous Vision: Art Appreciation in the Elementary Schools
Al Hurwitz and Hanley Madeja. Runhold, New York.
Understanding Childrens Art for better Teaching
Betty Lark Horovitz — Hilda Present Leivis and Mark Luca, Merrill Columbus, Ohio.
Preparation for Art
June King McFee. Wadswort California.
Analyzing Children's Art
Rhoda Kellogg Palo Alto, California National Press
Art Activity in the Primary School
Legmor Jennings. Hunman Educational Books Ltd. London 1973.
Art and Illusion
E.H. Gombrich Phardon, London.
The Story of Art
E.A. Gombrich Phardon, London.
Education through Art
Herbert Read. Faber and Faber, London.
Design Education: problem solving and visual experience
Peter Green. BT Batsford Ltd., London.